George A. Woodward

Philadelphia and Its Environs

A guide to the city and surroundings - Vol. 3

George A. Woodward

Philadelphia and Its Environs
A guide to the city and surroundings - Vol. 3

ISBN/EAN: 9783337193775

Printed in Europe, USA, Canada, Australia, Japan

Cover: Foto ©Andreas Hilbeck / pixelio.de

More available books at **www.hansebooks.com**

PHILADELPHIA

AND

ITS ENVIRONS.

A GUIDE TO

THE CITY AND SURROUNDINGS.

COLUMBIAN EDITION.

J. B. LIPPINCOTT COMPANY,
715 AND 717 MARKET STREET,
PHILADELPHIA.

STREETS AND HOUSE-NUMBERS.

In ascertaining the location of any residence or business-house in Philadelphia, it should be borne in mind that the city is divided into squares by two sets of streets crossing each other at right angles, one set running north and south parallel with the Delaware River, the other running east and west parallel with Market Street.

The numbering of the properties on the streets running north and south commences at Market Street, from which it extends both north and south; the numbering on the streets running east and west commences (on the line of Market Street) at Delaware Avenue on the Delaware River and extends westward to the west boundary of the city. In all cases the first number of each consecutive square commences a *new hundred*, regardless of the actual number last given in the preceding square. The following tables give the streets which mark the boundaries between the squares and illustrate the system of numbering. They also give the distance in miles and decimals of a mile of the principal streets severally from the starting-point, and thus enable the distance from street to street, or from one point to another, to be easily calculated.

Initial No. in the Square.	Principal Streets Running North and South.	Distance from Del. Ave.	Initial No. in the Square.	Principal Streets Running North and South.	Distance from Del. Ave.
1	Delaware Avenue	......	3400	Thirty-fourth Street	2.71
100	Front Street	.06+	3500	Thirty-fifth Street	2.80
200	Second Street	.15—	3600	Thirty-sixth Street	2.85+
300	Third Street	.25+	3700	Thirty-seventh Street	2.96—
400	Fourth Street	.34—	3800	Thirty-eighth Street	3.06
500	Fifth Street	.42	3900	Thirty-ninth Street	3.15—
600	Sixth Street	.51—	4000	Fortieth Street	3.27+
700	Seventh Street	.59	4100	Forty-first Street	3.39
800	Eighth Street	.68—	4200	Forty-second Street	3.49+
900	Ninth Street	.76—	4300	Forty-third Street	3.60—
1000	Tenth Street	.84+	4400	Forty-fourth Street	3.68+
1100	Eleventh Street	.93—	4500	Forty-fifth Street	3.77—
1200	Twelfth Street	1.05—	4600	Forty-sixth Street	3.87+
1300	Thirteenth Street	1.10—	4700	Forty-seventh Street	3.98—
1400	Broad [Fourteenth] Street	1.22—	4800	Forty-eighth Street	4.08—
1500	Fifteenth Street	1.32	4900	Forty-ninth Street	4.17—
1600	Sixteenth Street	1.39—	5000	Fiftieth Street	4.28+
1700	Seventeenth Street	1.47+	5100	Fifty-first Street	4.39—
1800	Eighteenth Street	1.56—	5200	Fifty-second Street	4.49+
1900	Nineteenth Street	1.64+	5300	Fifty-third Street	4.60
2000	Twentieth Street	1.72+	5400	Fifty-fourth Street	4.70—
2100	Twenty-first Street	1.83—	5500	Fifty-fifth Street	4.82+
2200	Twenty-second Street	1.91+	5600	Fifty-sixth Street	4.93—
2300	Twenty-third Street	1.98—	5700	Fifty-seventh Street	5.03+
2400	Twenty-fourth Street	2.00—	5800	Fifty-eighth Street	5.14—
......	*Schuylkill River*	......	5900	Fifty-ninth Street	5.24+
3000	Thirtieth Street	2.28—	6000	Sixtieth Street	5.35—
3100	Thirty-first Street	2.38—	6100	Sixty-first Street	5.45+
3200	Thirty-second Street	2.47—	6200	Sixty-second Street	5.56—
3300	Thirty-third Street	2.60+	6300	Sixty-third Street	5.67+

(OVER.)

STREETS AND HOUSE-NUMBERS.—CONTINUED.

Initial No. in the Square.	Principal Streets North of Market Street.	Distance from Market St.	Initial No. in the Square.	Principal Streets South of Market Street.	Distance from Market St.
100	Arch Street	0.16—	100	Chestnut Street	0.10+
200	Race Street	0.28+	.....	Sansom Street	.....
300	Vine Street	0.41+	200	Walnut Street	0.21—
400	Callowhill Street	0.52+	.....	Locust Street	0.28+
500	Buttonwood Street	0.65+	300	Spruce Street	0.37+
.....	Spring Garden Street	.....	400	Pine Street	0.47+
600	Green Street	0.81+	500	Lombard Street	0.53+
.....	Mount Vernon Street	0.86—	600	South Street	0.60+
.....	Wallace Street	0.90—	700	Bainbridge Street	0.67—
700	Fairmount Avenue	1.04—	.....	Fitzwater Street	.....
800	Brown Street	1.09+	800	Catharine Street	0.80+
.....	Parrish Street	1.17+	900	Christian Street	0.86—
900	Poplar Street	1.26—	1000	Carpenter Street	0.92+
1200	Girard Avenue	1.35—	1100	Washington Avenue	1.01+
1300	Thompson Street	1.47—	1200	Federal Street	1.16—
1400	Master Street	1.56—	1300	Wharton Street	1.27—
1500	Jefferson Street	1.65	1400	Reed Street	1.35+
1600	Oxford Street	1.75	1500	Dickinson Street	1.44—
1700	Columbia Avenue	1.85	1600	Tasker Street	1.52+
1800	Montgomery Avenue	1.96—	1700	Morris Street	1.63—
1900	Berks Street	2.05	1800	Moore Street	1.69+
2000	Norris Street	2.16—	1900	Mifflin Street	1.78—
2100	Diamond Street	2.27—	2000	McKean Street	1.86+
2200	Susquehanna Avenue	2.38—	2100	Snyder Avenue	1.95+
2300	Dauphin Street	2.50—	2200	Jackson Street	2.03+
2400	York Street	2.60—	2300	Wolf Street	2.12+
2500	Cumberland Street	2.70—	2400	Ritner Street	2.21+
2600	Huntingdon Street	2.80	2500	Porter Street	2.30—
2700	Lehigh Avenue	2.92—	2600	Shunk Street	2.38+
2800	Somerset Street	3.02—	2700	Oregon Avenue	2.48+
2900	Cambria Street	3.13—	2800	Johnson Street	2.57+
3000	Indiana Avenue	3.23	2900	Bigler Street	2.65—
3100	Clearfield Street	3.34—	3000	Pollock Street	2.73—
3200	Alleghany Avenue	3.45+	3100	Packer Street	2.83+
3300	Westmoreland Street	3.56—	3200	Curtin Street	2.92—
3400	Ontario Street	3.66—	3300	Geary Street	.....
3500	Tioga Street	3.77—	3400	Hartranft Street	.....
3600	Venango Street	3.87+	3500	Hoyt Street	.....
3700	Erie Street	3.99—	4300	League Island	3.87+

CONTENTS.

	PAGE
Introduction, Descriptive and Historical	7
Hotels, Theatres, Newspapers, Railroads, etc.	15

PRINCIPAL ATTRACTIONS IN AND AROUND THE CITY.

SECTION		PAGE
I.	The City Hall and Vicinity	19
II.	The Post-Office and Vicinity	46
III.	Independence Hall and Vicinity	56
IV.	Washington Square and Vicinity	73
V.	Franklin Square and Vicinity	78
VI.	Rittenhouse Square and Vicinity	83
VII.	Logan Square and Vicinity	93
VIII.	Broad and Locust Streets and Vicinity	102
IX.	South Broad Street and Vicinity	108
X.	Naval Asylum and Vicinity	115
XI.	Broad and Spring Garden Streets and Vicinity	119
XII.	North Broad Street and Vicinity	125
XIII.	Girard College and Vicinity	133
XIV.	Central Delaware-River Front and Vicinity	139
XV.	South Delaware-River Front and Vicinity	148
XVI.	North Delaware-River Front and Vicinity	152
XVII.	Delaware River North and South of the City	160
XVIII.	South West-Philadelphia	164

CONTENTS.

SECTION		PAGE
XIX.	North West-Philadelphia	173
XX.	Fairmount Water-Works and Vicinity	179
XXI.	East Fairmount Park and Vicinity	185
XXII.	West Fairmount Park and Vicinity	188
XXIII.	Laurel Hill Cemetery and Beyond	195
XXIV.	Up the Wissahickon	201
XXV.	The Reading Railroad's Routes	208
XXVI.	The Pennsylvania Railroad's Routes	216
XXVII.	To Camden and Beyond	227

PHILADELPHIA AND ITS ENVIRONS.

INTRODUCTION, DESCRIPTIVE AND HISTORICAL.

HILADELPHIA, the chief city of Pennsylvania, and one of the three cities of America and the nine cities of the world with more than a million inhabitants, while in industrial importance it has few rivals, is admirably situated on a low-lying peninsula between the Delaware and Schuylkill Rivers, near their junction, and ninety-six miles from the ocean, the Delaware affording it, by its width and depth, excellent commercial facilities. The closely built-up section of the city covers a nearly level tract of not over forty-six feet in its greatest height, though a much greater elevation is reached in the suburban section, a height of four hundred and forty feet being attained in the northern suburb. The municipal limits are very extensive, embracing an area of eighty-two thousand six hundred and three acres, or about one hundred and twenty-nine square miles, the city being twenty-two miles in extreme length and from five to ten miles in width. About one-eighth of this area is closely covered with buildings, while in the rural sections are a number of partly-detached towns and villages, and a multitude of handsome suburban residences.

The city is laid out in a strikingly regular manner, the streets crossing each other at right angles, part of them running east and west, from river to river, and part north and south, parallel to the Delaware. This plan is said to have been taken by William Penn from that of the city of Babylon. The north and south streets are known by numbers, running from First, or Front, Street to Sixty-third Street,—Fourteenth Street, midway between the rivers, being generally known as Broad Street. The east and west streets of the original city were named from the trees of the province, such as Chestnut, Walnut, Spruce, Pine, etc., though this rule applies now to only a few streets. The general width of these streets is about fifty feet, though there are several of a hundred feet and more in width. The system of paving has hitherto been an undesirable one, cobble-stones being generally used. These are now being rapidly replaced with granite block, asphalt, and other improved pavements. There are on the city plans about two thousand miles of streets. Of these more than one thousand miles are opened, and seven hundred and twenty-five miles had been paved by 1890. During the four years preceding 1891 improved pavements were laid on one hundred and twenty-seven miles of streets, much of this distance consisting of old streets repaved. This work is now going on with still greater rapidity, and if continued at the present rate the greater part, if not the whole, of the cobble-stone pavements will have disappeared by the year 1900.

Of the wider streets of Philadelphia, the leading north and south example is Broad Street, one hundred and thirteen feet wide, and opened for a length of some twelve miles. It is paved through several miles of its length with sheet asphaltum, and affords a magnificent avenue for carriages and processions. East and west through the centre of the city runs Market Street, one hundred feet wide and six miles long, its eastern portion being devoted to heavy wholesale business. Of the remaining wide avenues may be named Spring Garden Street, lined with handsome residences, and the favorite southern driveway to the Park; Fairmount, Girard, and Columbia Avenues; and Diamond Street, the principal northern carriage-road to the Park. Of the business streets, Chestnut and Eighth Streets stand first in retail trade, while Second Street is said to enjoy the distinction of being the longest street continuously lined with stores in the world. The rectangular character of the streets is broken by a few streets which run diagonally, and there has recently been placed on the city plan a diagonal Boulevard, one hundred and sixty feet in width, to run from the City Hall to Fairmount Park, and designed to be lined with buildings of imposing architecture, and to form an avenue of exceptional beauty.

Nearly every important street has its passenger railway—horse or cable—modes of propulsion, which are likely soon to be supplanted by electric motors. The total length of street railway is over three hundred miles. The ease of access which this gives to the centre of the city is added to by the railroads, which now run by elevated tracks to the heart of the business section, giving easy and rapid access from the suburban districts to the vicinity of the City Hall.

Philadelphia is notably a "city of homes." The tenement-house, so common elsewhere, is scarcely known within its precincts, its prevailing rule being one house for one family. No other city in the world contains so many comfortable single residences, largely owned by their occupants, great numbers of them being neat two-story structures, suitable for artisans, each with its bath-room and other modern conveniences. These houses are, as a rule, of brick, the abundance of brick-clay in the soil of the city making this the cheapest building material. Its long rows of red-brick walls and white-marble steps and sills gave the city formerly a very monotonous aspect. Of recent years, however, the architecture in the business and leading residence streets, and in the newer portions of the city, has greatly improved and become much varied, both in materials and style, so that in examples of striking and effective modern architecture Philadelphia can now vie with any city in the country. It is no less notable for the great number of charitable institutions, devoted to the most varied purposes, within its limits. A perusal of the following pages will show the existence of a multitude of hospitals, homes, orphanages, asylums, dispensaries, endowed schools, and other establishments partly or wholly supported by charity, which are but the most prominent among a host of such institutions, and speak well for the "quality of mercy" in the good city of "Brotherly Love."

The people of Philadelphia dwelt, in 1890, in about one hundred and eighty-seven thousand houses. The population at that time was 1,046,964, making an average of about 5.6 persons to a dwelling. It is doubtful if this low average is equalled by any other large city in the world. That of New York is more than three times as great. Since that date the city has been growing at the rate of about twelve thousand new houses, covering about one square mile of territory, annually, a rate which indicates an annual increase of about sixty thousand in population.

What is above said of the average of population to dwellings may be said with equal truth of the health record, the average death-rate being a very low one. This is, no doubt, largely due to the unusually free use of water, and the cleanliness which must thence result. The city is supplied with water principally from the Schuylkill River. Until recently its reservoirs had a total capacity of less than two hundred million gallons. There have, within a few years, been added the East Park and the Roxborough Reservoirs, giving a total capacity of over one billion gallons, which will be in the near future increased to one billion four hundred million gallons, by a reservoir projected at an elevated point known as Schuetzen Park. The present pumping capacity of the various stations is over two hundred million gallons daily, and the water annually stored amounts to about fifty billion gallons. The use of water by the citizens of Philadelphia is largely in excess of that of other cities, being at present over one hundred and fifty million gallons daily, or one hundred and forty gallons for every inhabitant of the city. This is nearly double the amount used in New York per inhabitant. During the summer months of 1892 the consumption averaged one hundred and eighty million gallons daily.

Philadelphia owns its own gas-works, which are extensive, and, under the present city government, are economically administered. The daily manufacturing capacity of the works is about twenty million cubic feet, which is more than double the average consumption. The maximum daily consumption reaches about fifteen million cubic feet. The use of gas is being reduced by the rapid extension of the electric light, many of the leading streets being now supplied with arc lights, while numerous stores, hotels, and other buildings are lighted by incandescent plants. Philadelphia was the first city to solve the problem of supplying high-tension arc lights from underground wires. Spring Garden, Green, Arch, and other streets are lighted without recourse to the deadly overhead wire.

William Penn, on laying out the city, made provision for five open squares, or small parks, as breathing-places. Subsequently several others were added. Recently there has been an active movement in this direction, several new open squares have been laid out, and a number of others, at suitable points, will soon be opened. In park facilities, in fact, Philadelphia surpasses any other city in America. Fairmount Park, with its area of nearly twenty-eight hundred acres, has no counterpart for size on this continent, and in picturesque beauty has no equal among the parks of the world. It has the unusual advantage of embracing the rolling and wooded banks of a large river; the Schuylkill, bordered by attractive bluffs and ravines, flowing for five miles within its confines. Here nature has provided numerous charming views and many localities of the highest rural beauty. In its Wissahickon extension it possesses as many miles of scenery as wild and grand as that of a mountain ravine. On the whole, Philadelphia can justly be proud of her unrivalled Park.

The railroad accommodations of Philadelphia are exceptionally good. The various railroads, which formerly had their terminal stations at points remote from the centre of the city, have been consolidated, and now reach central stations by elevated roadways, the Pennsylvania system having its terminus at Broad and Market Streets; the Reading system, at Twelfth and Market. The remaining road, the Baltimore and Ohio, reaches its station at Chestnut and Twenty-fourth Streets by a practically underground track. A Belt Line, to connect these roads and extend along the water front of the city, is about to be laid.

Facilities for navigation are equally good. The city has, on the Delaware, a river front of twenty miles in length, of which more than five miles are occupied by continuous wharves. On the Schuylkill, to Fairmount Dam, there are eight miles of navigable water, with four miles of wharves on the two sides of the river. The Delaware is broad and deep opposite the city, and is navigable throughout the year for vessels of the heaviest burden, while the accommodation for shipping is excellent, the average depth of water at the city wharves being fifty feet. The islands which occupy the centre of the river opposite the city, and have been a serious obstruction to navigation, are now being removed, the result of which will be to give Philadelphia one of the best harbors in the country. On their removal, the wharf lines, which have become inconveniently short for the great vessels of modern commerce, will be extended into the river on both sides, so as to deepen the water at the pier-heads and narrow the channel, thus preventing the formation of new bars or islands. The Schuylkill is navigable for craft of small burden, and is the seat of a considerable commerce, principally in petroleum and grain. This stream is crossed by many bridges, there being eighteen or more within the city limits, several of them being striking examples of engineering. The "double-decked" Spring Garden Street Bridge and the remarkably wide Girard Avenue Bridge are particularly notable.

The commercial and industrial interests of Philadelphia are of high importance. At one time its commerce was the most extensive of any city in the country. Though now surpassed in this respect by several other cities, it still has an annual ocean commerce of about $100,000,000 in exports and imports, and a very considerable internal commerce. It is to its manufactures, however, that Philadelphia owes its chief importance. In this field of industry it is preëminent in America, and is surpassed by few, if any, cities in the world, the annual product of its workshops being valued at about $600,000,000. Of the substances produced, the most prominent are iron and steel goods, woollen, worsted, and upholstery fabrics, and refined sugar, the value of these being about one-third of the whole. The remainder includes an immense variety of articles.

Philadelphia—the city of "Brotherly Love," or the "Quaker City," to give it its familiar titles—was founded in 1682, by William Penn, as the capital city of his new province of Pennsylvania. Its site had been occupied for many years before by Swedish colonists, of whose claims Penn made an equitable adjustment. The new inhabitants were members of the Society of Friends, or Quakers, to which sect the proprietor belonged, and descendants of whom still form an important element of the population. For one hundred and seventeen years this "green country town," as it had been called, continued the capital of Pennsylvania, and it grew so rapidly in population that throughout the colonial period, and long afterwards, it was the most important town, politically, commercially, and socially, on American soil. The first printing-press in the colonies was set up here in 1685. In 1723 came to Philadelphia its most distinguished citizen, Benjamin Franklin, to whose enterprise the city owes several of its notable institutions, such as the University of Pennsylvania, the American Philosophical Society, and the Philadelphia Library.

The old Assembly or State House of the province, completed in 1735, stands first among the historical monuments of our country. Here, on the 4th of July, 1776, was adopted that Declaration of Independence which first converted the colonies into a nation, and in the same building, in 1787, assembled the Convention which framed that Constitution of the United States under which this nation has gained its present eminence. This venerable edifice has long been known as Independence Hall.

Philadelphia was, with brief exceptions, the seat of the United States Government from the meeting of the First Congress, in 1774, until the establishment of Washington as the seat of government in 1800. Washington's "Farewell Address" to the people of the United States was delivered in this city, and here the "Father of his Country" retired from public life. Here, in 1781, was founded the first bank in the United States,—the Bank of North America,—and in 1792 the first mint for the coinage of money of the United States. The Protestant Episcopal Church of North America was organized here in 1786. Here also was founded, in 1791, the original Bank of the United States, and at a later date that subsequent Bank whose suppression by President Jackson precipitated a period of disaster upon the country.

Philadelphia continued the most populous city in the country till near 1830, when New York took the lead. The original city, as laid out under Penn's directions, was of narrow dimensions, being two miles—from the Delaware to the Schuylkill—east and west, and one mile—from Vine to Cedar (now South) Street—north and south; its centre being at Broad and Market Streets, the locality now occupied by the City Hall. Long before this space was filled with buildings there had grown up outlying settled districts, known by the various titles of Southwark, Northern Liberties, Kensington, Spring Garden, Moyamensing, Penn, Richmond, West Philadelphia, and Belmont; each of which had its own local government. Beyond these were the boroughs of Germantown, Manayunk, Frankford, etc., and a number of rural townships which embraced the remainder of the county. On the 2d of February, 1854, a Consolidation Act was passed by the State Legislature which extended the limits of the city to the county boundaries, and brought all these outlying districts under a single municipal government.

Of recent events in the history of Philadelphia the most important was the holding here of the Centennial World's Fair, commemorative of the signing of the Declaration of Independence. The display made was one that has been rarely surpassed, and it proved a highly useful object lesson to the people of the whole country. Later events of interest were the bi-centennial celebration of the landing of William Penn, in 1882, and the centennial celebration of the signing of the Constitution, in 1887, in which the military and industrial parades were of a grandeur rarely equalled.

In April, 1887, a new charter was granted to the city, which greatly increased the executive power of the mayor, and consolidated the various municipal departments under the heads of Public Works, Public Safety, Charities and Correction, Finance, Law, and Education, much to the advantage of the efficient government of the city. The directors of the first three named departments are appointed by the mayor, the official heads of the financial and law departments are elected, while the members of the Board of Education are appointed by the judges. The new system has greatly enhanced the harmony and economy of public operations.

Much has been said in recent years of the "New Philadelphia," and those whose knowledge of the city extends back two or three decades cannot but perceive that the term is well applied. A new and far more effective government, a stately City Hall, built for the needs of a century to come, a great improvement in the architecture and the condition of the streets of the city, largely increased water reservoirs and pumping machinery, rapid extension of electric lighting, central railroad termini, with the finest stations in the country, a magnificent exchange or bourse building, numerous other great public and private edifices, greatly developed educational institutions, much-improved navigation facilities, an exceptionally rapid growth in the products of manufacture, active measures for the development of commerce, etc., and with all this a steady reduction of debt and an adoption of the sound principle of keeping expenses within receipts, are but part of the improvements which the city has gained during the past two decades, and are full of promise for the future history of the **New Philadelphia**.

HOTELS, THEATRES, NEWSPAPERS, RAILROADS, ETC.

For the convenience of strangers visiting Philadelphia the description of places of interest is here preceded by a list of the leading hotels of the city (with their rates of board), the theatres and the daily newspapers, with location, the railroads, with offices, etc.

HOTELS.

Aldine Hotel. 1914 Chestnut Street. Terms: $3.50 to $5.00 per day.
Bellevue Hotel. N. W. corner Broad and Walnut Streets. European plan [without meals]. $2.00 per day and upwards.
Bingham House. Market and Eleventh Streets. Terms: $2.00 per day.
Colonnade Hotel. Chestnut and Fifteenth Streets. Terms: $3.50 per day and upwards. European plan, $1.00 and upwards.
Continental Hotel. Chestnut and Ninth Streets. Terms: $3.00 to $4.00 per day.
Dooner's Hotel. No. 23 South Tenth Street. European plan. $1.00 to $1.50 per day.
Girard House. Chestnut, east of Ninth Street. Terms: $3.00 per day.
Green's Hotel. Chestnut and Eighth Streets. European plan. $1.00 to $1.50 per day.
Hotel Brunswick. No. 40 North Broad Street. Terms: $2.00 per day. European plan, 75 cents to $1.50 per day.
Hotel Du Pont. No. 250 South Ninth Street. Terms: $2.00 per day.
Hotel Lafayette. Broad and Sansom Streets. Terms: $3.00 to $4.00 per day. European plan, $1.00 to $2.00 per day.
Hotel Vendig. Market and Twelfth Streets. European plan. $1.00 to $2.50 per day.
Irving House. No. 915 Walnut Street. Terms: $2.00 to $2.50 per day.
Keystone Hotel. No. 1524 Market Street. European plan. 50 cents to $1.25 per day.
Mansion House. No. 621 Arch Street. Terms: $2.00 per day.

Palmer House. No. 1607 Chestnut Street. Terms: $2.00 per day.
St. Charles Hotel. No. 60 North Third Street. Terms: $1.50 per day. European plan, 50 cents to 75 cents per day.
St. Elmo Hotel. No. 317 Arch Street. Terms: $2.00 per day.
Stratford Hotel. S. W. corner Broad and Walnut Streets. European plan, special rates.
Washington Hotel. No. 713 Chestnut Street. Terms: $2.00 to $2.50 per day.
Waverley Hotel. Fifteenth and Filbert Streets. European plan. 50 cents to $3.00 per day.
Windsor Hotel. No. 1217 Filbert Street. Terms: $2.00 to $2.50 per day. European plan, $1.00 to $1.50 per day.
Zeisse's Hotel. No. 820 Walnut Street. European plan. $1.00 to $2.00 per day.

THEATRES.

Academy of Music. S. W. corner Broad and Locust Streets. Operas, Concerts, Lectures, etc.
Arch Street Theatre. No. 613 Arch Street. Dramatic Entertainments.
Bijou Theatre. No. 215 North Eighth Street. Variety Performances.
Broad Street Theatre. No. 225 South Broad Street. Dramatic and Operatic Entertainments.
Carncross's Opera House. No. 19 South Eleventh Street. Minstrel Performances.
Chestnut Street Opera House. No. 1025 Chestnut Street. Dramatic Entertainments.
Chestnut Street Theatre. No. 1211 Chestnut Street. Dramatic and Operatic Entertainments.
Palace Theatre. No. 1005 Arch Street. Minor Drama and Opera.
Dime Museum. Arch and Ninth Streets. Living Curiosities, etc.
Empire Theatre. S. E. corner Broad and Locust Streets. Dramatic and Variety Entertainments.
Forepaugh's Theatre. No. 255 North Eighth Street. Dramatic Performances.
Girard Avenue Theatre. Girard Avenue, near Seventh Street. Dramatic Performances.
Germania Theatre. No. 532 North Third Street. German Drama.
Grand Opera House. Broad Street and Montgomery Avenue. Summer and Winter Opera.

Kellar's Egyptian Hall. Chestnut, above Twelfth Street. Sleight-of-hand Performances and mechanical illusions.
Kensington Theatre. East Norris Street and Frankford Avenue. Dramatic Performances.
Lyceum Theatre. No. 729 Vine Street. Minor Drama.
Musical Fund Hall. No. 806 Locust Street. Concerts, Lectures, etc.
National Theatre. Ridge Avenue and Tenth Street. Dramatic Entertainments.
Park Theatre. Broad Street and Fairmount Avenue. Dramatic Entertainments.
People's Theatre. Kensington Avenue and Cumberland Street. Minor Drama.
Standard Theatre. No. 1126 South Street. Minor Drama.
Star Theatre. Eighth, above Race Street. Minor Drama.
Walnut Street Theatre. Walnut and Ninth Streets. Dramatic Entertainments.
Winter Circus. Broad and Cherry Streets. Circus Performances.

DAILY NEWSPAPERS.

Bulletin, Evening. No. 607 Chestnut Street. Republican.
Call (Evening). No. 26 South Seventh Street. Independent.
Democrat, Philadelphia (Morning). No. 612 Chestnut Street. Democratic (German).
German Gazette (Morning). Race and Seventh Streets. Independent (German).
Herald, Evening. No. 21 South Seventh Street. Democratic.
Inquirer, Philadelphia (Morning). No. 929 Chestnut Street. Republican.
Item, Evening. No. 28 South Seventh Street. Independent.
Ledger, Public (Morning). Chestnut and Sixth Streets. Independent.
News, Daily (Morning and Evening). No. 29 South Seventh Street. Independent Republican.
North American (Morning). Chestnut and Seventh Streets. Republican.
Press, Philadelphia (Morning). Chestnut and Seventh Streets. Republican.
Record, Philadelphia (Morning). No. 917 Chestnut Street. Democratic.

Star, Evening. No. 30 South Seventh Street. Independent.
Telegraph, Evening. No. 108 South Third Street. Republican.
Tageblatt (Morning). No. 613 Callowhill Street. Independent (German).
Times (Morning). Chestnut and Eighth Streets. Independent.
Volks-blatt (Morning). No. 23 South Seventh Street. Democratic (German).

RAILROADS, TELEGRAPHS, ETC.

Baltimore and Ohio Railroad. Routes to Wilmington, Baltimore, and the West; to New York, via Reading Railroad. Station, Twenty-fourth and Chestnut Streets. Ticket offices at station, at N. E. corner Broad and Chestnut, N. E. corner Ninth and Chestnut, and No. 609 South Third Street.

Pennsylvania Railroad. Routes to New York, Germantown, Schuylkill Valley, Harrisburg and Pittsburg, Media and West Chester, Wilmington and Baltimore, etc.; station, Broad and Market Streets. To Atlantic City, Cape May, etc.; station, Market Street Wharf. Ticket-offices at stations, at S. E. corner Broad and Chestnut, and S. E. corner Ninth and Chestnut Streets.

Philadelphia and Reading Railroad. Routes to New York, Germantown and Chestnut Hill, Bethlehem, Reading, Harrisburg, etc.; station, Twelfth and Market Streets. To Atlantic City and Southern New Jersey; stations, Chestnut Street and South Street Wharves. Ticket-offices at stations, at N. E. corner Broad and Chestnut, N. E. corner Ninth and Chestnut Streets, No. 609 South Third Street.

American District Telegraph Company. Main office, No. 113 South Broad Street; district offices, N. E. corner Broad and Chestnut, No. 106 South Eighth Street, and elsewhere throughout the city.

Western Union Telegraph Company. Offices, S. E. corner Third and Chestnut, S. W. corner Tenth and Chestnut, S. E. corner Broad and Chestnut Streets, at hotels, railroad stations, etc.

Postal Telegraph Cable Company. Office, N. E. corner Third and Chestnut Streets.

Bell Telephone Company. Central station, No. 408 Market Street.

Adams Express Company. Offices, N. W. corner Seventeenth and Market, S. W. corner Broad and Chestnut, and S. W. corner Fourth and Chestnut Streets.

United States Express Company. Office, No. 624 Chestnut Street.

PRINCIPAL ATTRACTIONS IN AND AROUND THE CITY.

I.

THE CITY HALL AND VICINITY.

CONSPICUOUS among the numerous architectural attractions of Philadelphia is the new **City Hall** (popularly known as "The Public Buildings"), standing at the intersection of Broad and Market Streets, on the plot of ground once known as Penn Square, sufficiently near the geographical centre of the city to be easy of access from all sections, and marking a locality that is rapidly becoming noted for its attractive business establishments. This enormous structure, which was begun on the 10th of August, 1871, is probably the largest building in America, not excepting the Capitol at Washington, being four hundred and eighty-six and one-half feet in length, north and south, and four hundred and seventy in width, east and west, covering an area of four and one-half acres, exclusive of a court-yard in the centre two hundred feet square. Around the whole is a grand avenue, two hundred and five feet wide on the northern front and one hundred and thirty-five feet on the others. The basement-story of this building is of fine granite, and the superstructure of white marble from the Lee (Massachusetts) quarries, the whole strongly backed with brick and made thoroughly fire-proof. It contains five hundred and twenty rooms, and, besides the offices of the City Government, which are being concentrated here as rapidly as accommodations can be prepared for them, on the second floor at the south front of the building are the chambers of the **Supreme Court of Pennsylvania.** Surmounting this splendid structure is a central tower which rises to an altitude of five hundred and thirty-seven and one-third feet and terminates in a colossal statue of William Penn, thirty-six feet in height. Architecturally the City Hall is a highly ornate building, being a magnificent example of the French Renaissance, with its florid combination of classic and modern schools. Internally it is adorned with a large amount of statuary in high and low relief, while externally gigantic statues look down from the numerous lofty pediments. The entrances are imposingly grand, that on the northern side containing a series of magnificent polished-stone columns, while the hall under the great tower is unique and striking in its architectural effects. Externally, the lofty tower, of unrivalled height, is visible for miles in every direction. The edifice is one of which Philadelphia can justly be proud, since in dimensions it is by far the leading municipal building in America, and in height Europe has no building to equal it.

Flanking the new City Hall on the north, the **Masonic Temple**, whose corner-stone was laid in 1868, in the presence of ten thousand of the fraternity, rears its stately head high above the neighboring houses. It is built of granite dressed at the quarry and brought to the site ready to be raised at once to its place. Over $1,500,000 was expended in the construction of this edifice, which, in 1873, was dedicated with imposing ceremonies. The Temple is one hundred and fifty feet in breadth by two hundred and fifty in length, with a side elevation of ninety feet above the pavement, its colossal proportions making it seem low, even with this height. A tower two hundred and fifty feet high rises at one corner, while at other points minor towers and spires rise above the cornice, forming attractive ornaments to the several fronts of the structure. Ten lodge-rooms, of which three, the Norman, the Ionic, and the Egyptian Halls, are superbly decorated, with the richly-appointed Banquet Hall, and the Grand Master's apartments, constitute the principal features of the interior of the Temple. In addition to the rooms named are the Corinthian, the Renaissance, the Gothic, and the Oriental Halls, the architecture of each being in accordance with its name. Of the decorated halls, the Egyptian is of surpassing beauty and archæological correctness, that of London, hitherto deemed the finest in the world, being inferior to it. This magnificent Temple is the only one in this country which is exclusively devoted to Masonic purposes, and in grandeur of dimensions and artistic beauty of decoration it is said to have no equal among the Masonic Temples of the world.

North of the Masonic Temple, at the intersection of Broad and Arch Streets, stands a group of three handsome churches, Methodist, Baptist, and Lutheran, respectively of white marble, brown-stone, and green serpentine, which form a highly effective architectural feature of that locality. The marble spire of the Methodist church

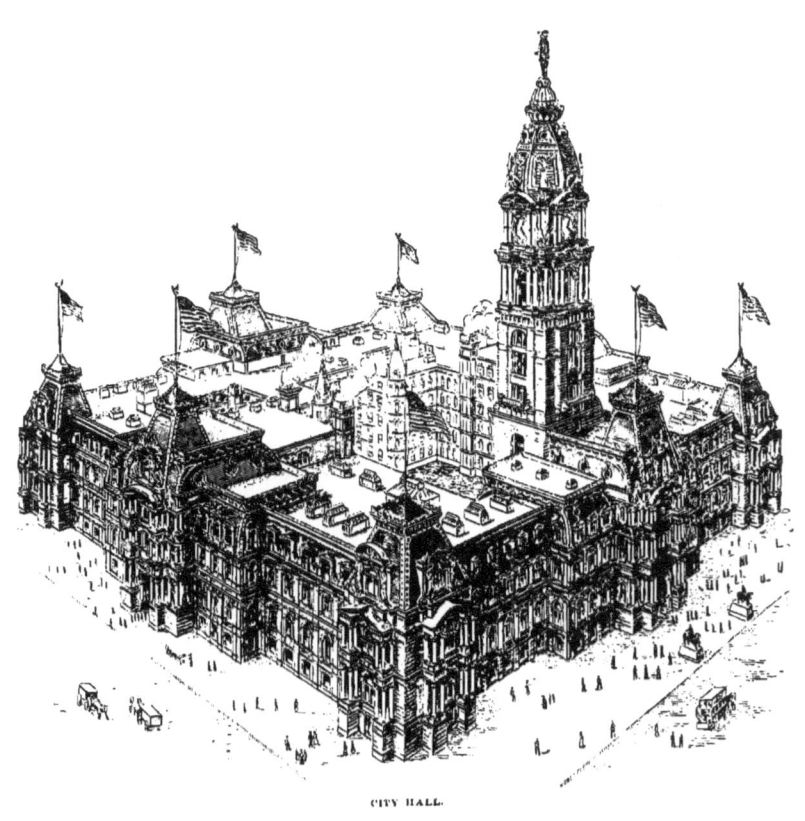

CITY HALL.

MASONIC TEMPLE.

is of exquisite beauty of proportions, while each of the other churches has its particular elements of attraction.

A short distance north of the City Hall, at the corner of Broad and Cherry Streets, stands the **Academy of Fine Arts**, in the Venetian style of architecture. The association to which this building belongs was founded in 1805, and incorporated under the name and style of the Pennsylvania Academy of the Fine Arts. Its first home was in a building which it erected on Chestnut Street above Tenth, where it began a series of exhibitions which continued, annually, for more than half a century. Its present fine structure was completed in 1876. The building presents on Broad Street a highly-ornate and striking façade, composed of a central tower and two slightly-recessed wings. Over the principal entrance is shrined a mutilated antique statue of the goddess Ceres, above which bends the arch of the great east window. The structure is one hundred by two hundred and sixty feet, and is practically fire-proof, no wood entering into its construction, except a thin lining on the walls to protect the pictures against dampness, a single thickness on some of the floors, and some doors and finishings; everything else is iron, brick, or stone, so that works of art placed within its walls are as safe as human care can make them. The roof is of iron, covered with slate and glass. The principal interior ornamentation of the building has been concentrated in the main entrance hall and staircase. The stone used in them is Ohio sandstone, from the Cleveland quarries; the shafts of the columns under the stairs are of Victoria and rose crystal marbles and Jersey granite, and those of the upper hall of Tennessee marble. The capitals of all the interior columns are of French Eschallon marble; the rail of the main staircase is of solid bronze. The cost of the building was nearly four hundred thousand dollars, and of the site ninety-five thousand dollars. Within this noble building is gathered one of the most extensive and, historically considered, the most interesting collection in the United States. It includes about three hundred oil-paintings, numerous bronzes, marbles, and sculptures, several hundred casts, and many thousand engravings, and besides these, which constitute its permanent museum, annual exhibitions are held of the works of contributing artists, and special loan exhibitions are arranged from time to time, generally from private galleries of wealthy citizens.

But the Academy of Fine Arts is something more than a splendid picture- and sculpture-gallery. It embraces a system of schools supported primarily in the interest of those who intend to become professional artists, besides whom those who expect to devote themselves to decorative painting and sculpture as a means of livelihood (lithographers, china-painters, decorators, etc.) are welcomed to the schools, as are also amateurs so far as is practicable without interference with the professional students. The Academy does not undertake to furnish detailed instruction, but, rather, facilities for study supplemented by the criticism of teachers. The classes consist of an antique, a life, a portrait, and modelling classes. Lectures on artistic anatomy are delivered twice a week, and the facilities for the study of anatomy are superior to those possessed by any other art school in the world. The artists represented by works in the Academy galleries include many of the most distinguished names, while the collection embraces such notable paintings as West's "Death on the Pale Horse," Wittkamp's "Deliverance of Leyden," Read's "Sheridan's Ride," Vanderlyn's "Ariadne of Naxos," Bouguereau's "Orestes pursued by the Furies," and others of equal note; and among its works of sculpture are Lough's "Battle of the Centaurs and the Lapithæ," Story's "Jerusalem," Rinaldini's "Penelope," Lombardi's "Deborah," Powers's "Proserpine," and Palmer's "Spring." The more recent treasures include the valuable Phillips collection of over forty thousand etchings and engravings, and the growing Temple gallery, now numbering thirty-two choice paintings. When to these shall be added the Henry C. Gibson bequest (not yet received) of one hundred of the best examples of modern paintings, some of them of inestimable value, the Academy collections will be second in artistic worth to no others in this country.

Opposite the Academy of Fine Arts, at the south-east corner of Broad and Cherry Streets, the new **Odd-Fellows' Hall**, now in process of erection, promises to add greatly to the architectural attractions of this section of the city. The building in which this Order has been housed for nearly fifty years back, on Sixth Street, below Race, has long proved inadequate to its purpose, and in 1888 the present site was purchased, with a front of one hundred and twenty feet on Broad Street and a depth of one hundred and seventy feet on Cherry Street. The new building will be fully adapted to the needs of the Order, and a beautiful example of the Italian Renaissance style of architecture, that which was so largely used in the stately mansions and public buildings of our colonial period, and which is again coming into

ODD-FELLOWS' HALL.

popular use. The edifice ascends to the height of nine stories, and is fire-proof throughout, the materials for its outer walls being marble for the three lower stories, and for the remainder buff Pompeian brick, with light-colored terra-cotta for the pilasters, cornices, and other ornamental details, the total effect being one of simplicity, beauty, and solidity. Internally, the first floor contains a large and handsomely-ornamented Grand Lodge room, suitable for lectures and other entertainments, rooms for the Grand Secretary, etc. The four succeeding floors will be rented out for offices, and the remaining floors of the lofty edifice are devoted to the purposes of the Order, there being in all fourteen large Lodge-rooms, two Encampment-rooms, and a Degree-room, with various other apartments. As a whole, this new home of the Odd-Fellows favorably compares with the massive dwelling of the Masonic Order in its vicinity, and as an instance of pure architecture testifies to the growing taste for nobler and more correct examples of this long-neglected art.

Located on Broad Street, above Race, and extending through to Fifteenth Street, is the **Hahnemann Medical College and Hospital,**

Hahnemann Medical College and Hospital.
the oldest and the leading Homœopathic institution in the country. The building of the college proper is a fine edifice in the modified Gothic style of architecture, with a front on Broad Street of seventy feet and a depth of one hundred feet, having a central tower terminating in a pyramidal spire. A series of hospital buildings join the college on the rear, embracing an out-patient or dispensary building, a public wards building, an administrative building, and a building for private wards and children's hospital. The institution was organized in 1848. Since that date the dispensary has given gratuitous medical treatment to more than three hundred thousand patients. The hospital, of recent completion, has been no less active in good work. There has recently been added to it a training-school for nurses. The college is prosperous, its matriculates for the last session having been two hundred and forty-seven in number.

At the north-east corner of Broad and Vine Streets, three squares north of the City Hall, is the new building of the **Roman Catholic**

Catholic High School.
High School, a beautiful marble structure, three stories in height, on a high granite base, surmounted by an appropriate tower, and having fronts on Vine and Broad Streets of one hundred and fifteen and one hundred and forty feet respectively. This institution is the outgrowth of a bequest of

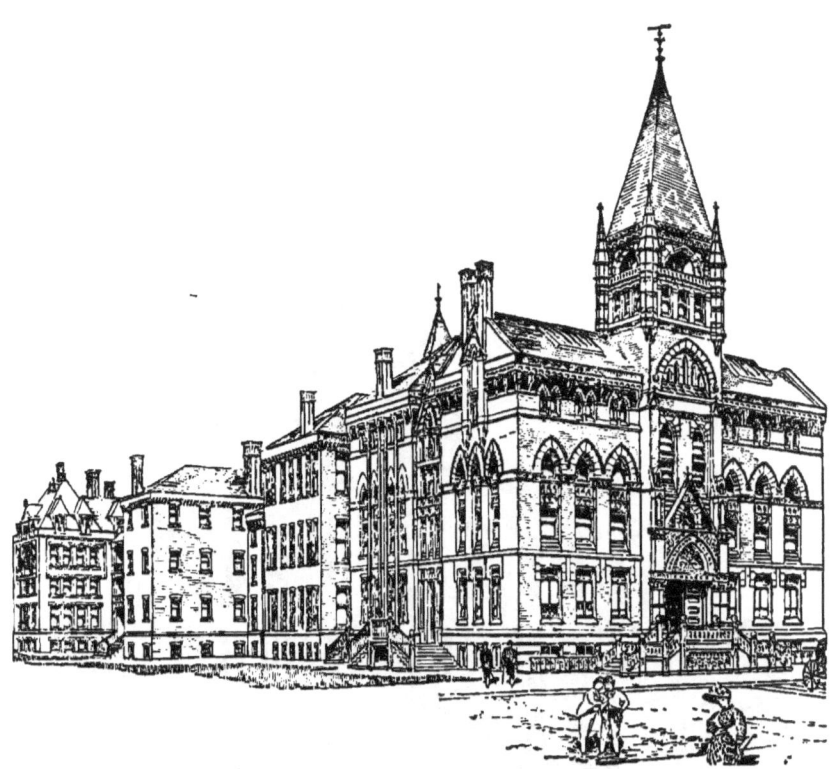

HAHNEMANN MEDICAL COLLEGE AND HOSPITAL.

ROMAN CATHOLIC HIGH SCHOOL.

Mr. Thomas E. Cahill, late president of the Knickerbocker Ice Company, and is intended to supplement the Catholic parochial schools by a course of semi-industrial instruction, particularly in the mechanical and scientific arts, with the view of securing for its pupils a practical rather than a classical education.

We may speak, in passing, of the **Muhr Building**, the principal jewelry manufactory of the city, at the south-west corner of Broad and Race Streets; nearly opposite which, at 145 North Broad Street, is the **Armory of the State Fencibles**, a battalion of the Pennsylvania militia.

Leaving Broad Street, we find on Race Street, west of Fifteenth, the **Hicksite Friends' Meeting** and the **Friends' Central School**, the latter an institution of excellent repute and well patronized. The

Friends' Meeting and School.

grounds extend to Cherry Street, the cool, shady lawn in front giving a comfortable aspect to the roomy brick meeting-house, which stands far back from the street. From Sixteenth to Seventeenth, Race to Cherry Streets, are grounds belonging to the Orthodox Friends, partly taken up by a disused graveyard, partly occupied by the **Friends' Select School** and the **Friends' Library**. The Library, on Sixteenth Street, is free to readers, and contains from ten thousand to twelve thousand books, exclusively on instructive subjects. In a fire-proof room of this building are stored the books of record of all the Meetings represented in the Philadelphia Yearly Meeting, which embraces New Jersey, Delaware, and the most of Pennsylvania. These have an important historical value.

On the opposite side of Broad Street, at Arch and Thirteenth Streets, stands the white marble edifice known as **St. George's Hall**,

St. George's Hall.

the head-quarters of the St. George Society, an association which dates back to 1772, its original purpose being to give advice and assistance to Englishmen in distress. The building has a handsome Ionic portico, surmounted by an effective bronze group of St. George and the Dragon. On the second floor is the large assembly hall of the Society. On the first floor are the rooms of the **Women's Christian Temperance Union**. There are a number of similar national societies in Philadelphia, including the German Society, the Welsh Society, the Hibernian Society, the St. Andrew's Society, and several others, most of them dating back to the last century, and all of combined social and charitable character.

Returning to the immediate vicinity of the City Hall, we find the

THE CITY HALL AND VICINITY.   31

Masonic Temple, its neighbor on the north, matched by several structures of an equally striking character. Facing the City Hall on the west may be seen the **Broad Street Station of the Pennsylvania Railroad**, whose original effective building is now being added to by

Pennsylvania Railroad Station.
one of immense proportions, which, when completed, will be ten stories in height (eight of them being used for the offices of the Company), and have, including the present building, a front of three hundred and seven feet on Broad Street (from Market to Filbert) and a depth extending sixty feet beyond Fifteenth Street. On the corner of Broad and Market Streets rises a stately and effective tower two hundred and forty feet in height, with at its base a grand main entrance. There is another entrance on Filbert Street, and excellent facilities for carriage entrance. On the second floor is a main waiting-room of spacious dimensions, dining-room, restaurant, and other conveniences for the army of travellers who daily pass through this station. The train-shed is being extended on the same grand scale, and when completed will be more than seven hundred feet long by three hundred and seven wide, being crossed by great iron arches with the unequalled span of two hundred and ninety-four feet. The floor of the train-shed will afford space for sixteen tracks, greatly increasing the facilities of the station, which, as a whole, will be the largest and handsomest railroad terminal in the world. From the train-shed an elevated road-bed, covered with a net-work of tracks, leads to an iron bridge which crosses the Schuylkill River, beyond which the several divisions of the road branch off in their proper directions. The space out Market Street to Eighteenth is covered by the great freight warehouses of the Company and by the offices and warehouse of the Adams Express Company, while much of that beyond is devoted to coal-yards and other purposes, the whole plant being one of unprecedented magnitude and perfection. This great station is a scene of almost momentarily arriving and departing trains, and hurrying passengers, of whom sixty thousand are said daily to use the station, while their numbers are steadily increasing.

Immediately south of the City Hall, on the east side of Broad Street, stands the lofty and imposing **Betz Building**, the most striking example of this class of edifice in the eastern section of the

Betz Building.
country. This magnificent structure has fronts of one hundred and four feet on Broad Street and one hundred feet on South Penn Square, and is one hundred and

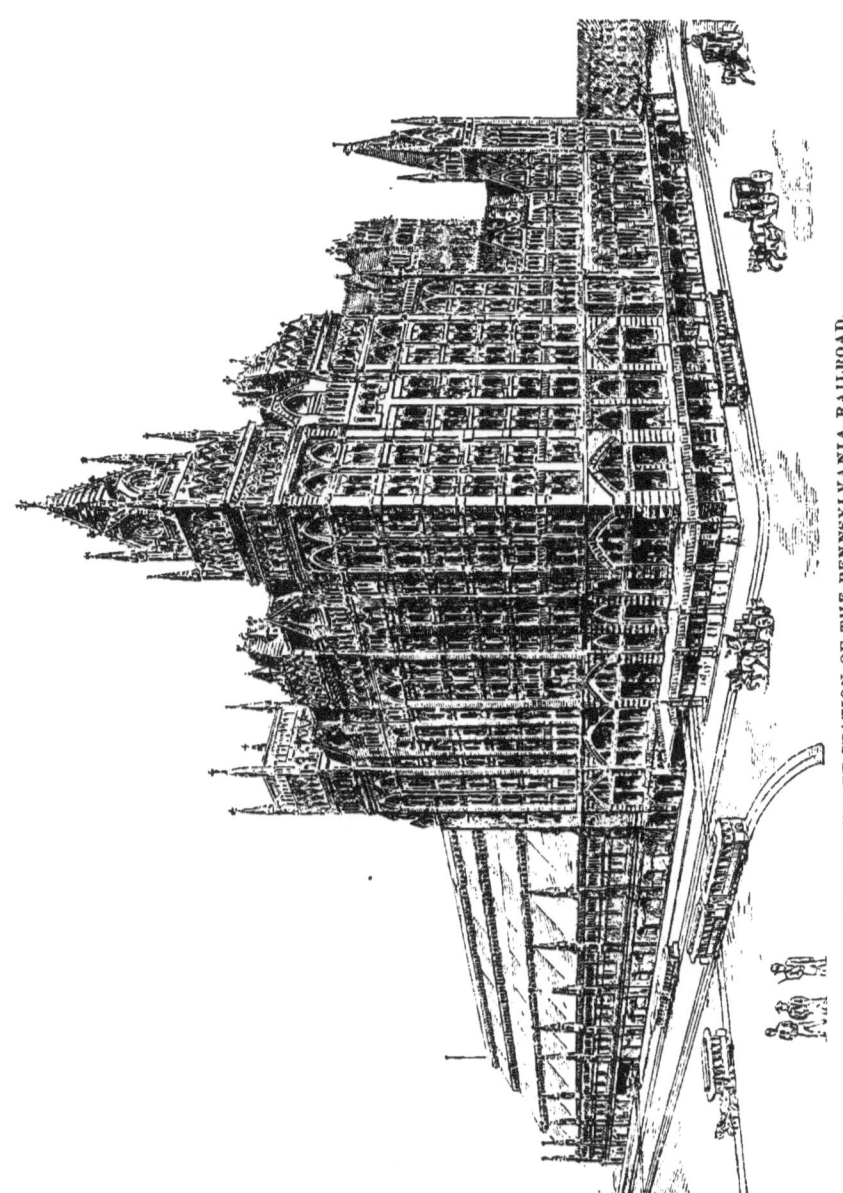

BROAD STREET STATION OF THE PENNSYLVANIA RAILROAD.

ninety-four feet high, having thirteen stories above the street, with deep basement and cellar. The street fronts are of granite to the top of the second story, and of Kentucky limestone above, the remaining walls being of buff brick. The style of architecture is the modern Romanesque, attractively ornamented, a peculiar feature of the ornamentation being a bronze cornice above the second-story windows, in which are heads of all the Presidents of the United States, from Washington to Harrison, the terms of each being indicated in the frieze. Interiorly the building is fire-proof, and is divided into three hundred and four office-rooms, oak finished, of ample size, and well-lighted. The entire building is heated by steam and lighted by electricity from plants in the cellar and basement.

Adjoining this building, at the north-east corner of Broad and Chestnut Streets, with a front of one hundred feet on the former and ninety-five feet on the latter, is the large and attractive edifice of the **Girard Life Insurance, Annuity, and Trust Company of Philadelphia**, incorporated in 1836, and, with a single exception, the oldest Trust Company in the State. The building is Romanesque in its general style of architecture, and is nine stories high, surmounted by a tower. A lofty arched entrance on Chestnut Street leads, through a hall adorned with richly-colored marbles, to the office of the Trust Company. The remainder of the building is occupied by offices. In this building are located the **University Law School** and the accompanying **Biddle Law Library**.

Girard Life and Trust Company.

At the south-west corner of Broad and Sansom Streets stands the house of the noted **Union League of Philadelphia**, which had its birth in the early years of the civil war and achieved a world-wide celebrity by its stanch support of the government in the crises of that period. Ten regiments of troops were enlisted under its auspices during the war; hundreds of thousands of Union documents were printed and distributed, and vast sums of money were freely contributed by its members in aid of the Union cause. The present building, opened in 1865, but since much enlarged as the wants of the club demanded, is a typical club-house of the better sort, embracing a spacious parlor, smoking-room, library, reading-room, banquet-room, billiard-room, assembly-room, private dining-rooms, and restaurant, all superbly adorned with frescoed ceilings and numerous paintings and pieces of statuary—the building and fittings aggregating a value of over $300,000.

Union League.

UNION LEAGUE CLUB HOUSE.

THE CITY HALL AND VICINITY. 35

Just below, at the corner of Broad and Walnut Streets, stands the **Bellevue Hotel**, noted for the excellence of its cuisine, and near at hand, on Walnut Street (No. 1409), and extending to Moravian Street, is the house of the **Manufacturers' Club**, a striking specimen of modern

Manufacturers' Club. architecture. Five stories in height (eighty-three feet to the cornice and one hundred feet to the tower finial), it reaches far above the adjoining buildings, while its front of stone, occupied principally by an extensive bay window of unique fashion, forms a curious contrast to the prevailing style of that section; somewhat less attractive, though still striking, is the bow-shaped Moravian Street front of pressed brick, the windows of which overlook the Union League house and grounds. The several rooms and halls of the Manufacturers' Club, reception-room, café, library, reading- and assembly-room, parlor, private and club dining-rooms, card-room, etc., are elaborately finished in old oak, mahogany, and sycamore, and handsomely furnished and decorated.

On Fifteenth Street, fronting on Chestnut and extending to Sansom, is the attractive building of the **Young Men's Christian Associa-**

Y. M. C. Association. tion, of which the ground floor is occupied by stores, and the upper stories are devoted to the purposes of the Association. The main entrance is on Fifteenth Street, from which stairs lead, on the right hand, to the popular **Association Hall**, so much in use for lectures and similar entertainments, and on the left to the reading- and assembly-rooms, parlor, library, gymnasium, and other apartments of the Association. The building is one of the best appointed for its purpose in the country.

In this vicinity are the head-quarters of several other religious associations. At 1420 Chestnut Street stands the stately building of the **Baptist Board of Publication**, in which are the rooms of the **Baptist Historical Society** and the offices of several denominational papers. At 1512 Chestnut Street are the rooms of the **American Tract Society**, and in this and the adjoining building are the offices of two leading Presbyterian newspapers. At 1334-1336 Chestnut Street is the extensive edifice of the **Presbyterian Board of Publication**, containing a book store, assembly- and committee-rooms, etc., and serving as the Philadelphia Presbyterian head-quarters. Farther east, at 1122 Chestnut Street, stands the granite building of another important religious institution, the **American Sunday-school Union**, erected in 1854, and constituting the central office of the Union, whose branches extend throughout the world. The Methodist denomination has its head-quarters at 1018 Arch Street, where are the **Methodist Bookrooms**, the literary and business centre of the Philadelphia Conference. Here is the office of the **Philadelphia Methodist**.

Fronting on Chestnut Street, east of Broad, stands the white marble building, with Ionic portico, which for sixty years has done duty as the **United States Mint**. The original Mint building, erected in 1792, on Seventh Street, above Market, was the first structure built in the United States under authority of the Federal Government. Proving inadequate, it was replaced by the present building, erected 1829-1833. For many years this served for all the purposes of United States coinage, and at the present day all the minor coins, and the devices and dies for all coins, are made here. This building has, in its turn, become too small, the 10,000,000 pieces coined here in 1833 having grown to 92,198,269 pieces in 1891. The value of the total coinage in Philadelphia in the century since the establishment of the Mint has been $1,056,337,771.05. The great increase in work has long pressed severely on the capacity of the establishment, and its replacement by a larger building has become necessary. Recently a bill passed Congress for the erection of a new Mint, for which the location between Sixth and Seventh, Walnut and Sansom Streets, facing Washington Square on the south and Independence Square on the east, has been decided upon. The near future will probably see Philadelphia provided with a building adequate for all demands for minting for many years to come, and architecturally an ornament to the city. The Mint is open during several hours of the day to visitors, and in addition to its manufacturing processes, possesses a valuable cabinet of ancient and modern coins.

United States Mint.

Facing the City Hall on the east, and occupying the square bounded by Chestnut, Market, Thirteenth, and Juniper Streets, stands the widely-known **Wanamaker Grand Depot**, a mercantile establishment of such extent, variety of goods, and brilliancy of display, that buyers and sight-seers alike regard it as one of Philadelphia's special attractions, and seek it as they might a constantly-changing fair. This extensive establishment is, in its retail department, four stories in height, counting the much-frequented basement, and embraces over fifty departments, in which merchandise of almost every kind is on sale, while four thousand employees attend to the wants of its patrons. In its particular line Wanamaker's is an institution perhaps without its equal in the world.

Wanamaker Grand Depot.

UNITED STATES MINT.

HALE BUILDING, 1326-1328 CHESTNUT STREET.

At the south-west corner of Chestnut and Juniper Streets stands the **Hale Building**, an edifice notable alike for its architecture and its history, it having been the home of the recently notorious Keystone National Bank, the scene of a defalcation and an abuse of public trust not likely soon to be forgotten in the annals of the Quaker City. The building is one of the handsomest structures in the city, being seven stories in height, surmounted by a tower; the Chestnut Street front of rock-faced Indiana limestone, the Juniper Street front an attractive combination of brick and terra-cotta, ornamented with projecting balconies of stone. The building is now occupied by the **Central Saving Fund, Trust, and Safe Deposit Company**, and by offices. Just above, at 1340 Chestnut Street, stands the small but unusually massive granite building of the **Real Estate Trust Company of Philadelphia**.

<small>Hale Building.</small>

On the south-west corner of Twelfth and Chestnut Streets is the edifice of the **Beneficial Saving-Fund Society**, six stories in height; the first story front of granite, the remainer of brick with granite trimmings. Opposite, on the south-east corner, is the five-storied building of the **S. S. White Dental Manufacturing Company**, the head-quarters of the largest dental instrument manufactory in the country. It has branch houses in New York, Brooklyn, Boston, and Chicago.

<small>Beneficial Saving-Fund.</small>

On Twelfth Street, below Chestnut (No. 124), is situated the recently-built home of the **New Century Club**, an association of ladies organized for the double purpose of social enjoyment and the public good, and which has wrought nobly for the cause of reform in Philadelphia. Founded in 1876, as its name indicates, we owe to it the origin of such important institutions as the **Children's Country Week** (an idea which has since been adopted by other cities), the **Working-Women's Guild**, and the **Cooking School**, all now separate and thriving associations. Still connected with it are the Working-Women's Legal Protection and the Police Matrons' Committees, which have done excellent work. Another outgrowth, of an intellectual cast, is the **Browning Society**. The new building was first occupied in 1892. It has an attractive front of Pompeian brick and terra-cotta, and internally is admirably adapted to club purposes. Its Drawing-room, or Assembly Hall, on the second floor, has become a favorite place for amateur theatricals, private balls, and other entertainments.

<small>New Century Club.</small>

An educational institution of much interest may be seen at Nos.

NEW CENTURY CLUB.

8-10 South Twelfth Street. This is the **William Penn Charter School**, which has the double celebrity of being the oldest chartered school in the United States and the largest boys' day's school of its class in the country. The first school in Philadelphia was established in 1683. This was succeeded in 1689 by a public school under the care of the celebrated George Keith, the direct progenitor of the present school, which has, therefore, had more than two centuries of continuous existence. It was chartered by William Penn in 1701, and again in 1708 and 1711, its purpose being the instruction of youth "in the principles of true religion and virtue, and qualifying them to serve their country and themselves." This school, although supported by the Quakers, was open to all, and for more than sixty years was the only public place for instruction in the province. For more than a century it was located on Fourth Street, below Chestnut. In its present location it has accommodations for more than three hundred and fifty boys, and possesses all the accessories of a completely-equipped school. Its historical interest, and its present high rank among schools of its class, make it well worthy the attention of visitors.

<small>Wm. Penn Charter School.</small>

On Market Street, with a front extending from Twelfth nearly to Eleventh Street, is the new **Terminal Station of the Philadelphia and Reading Railroad Company,** one of the most stately and imposing of the many recent architectural adornments of the city. The building is eight stories in height, the first and second stories being devoted to the use of the travelling public, while the others are used for offices of the Company and other purposes. The front is of massive granite for the first story and of terra-cotta and brick for the remaining stories, the order of architecture being the Italian Renaissance. The width on Market Street is two hundred and sixty-seven feet, the height one hundred and fifty-two feet. On the second, or main station, floor is a large passenger waiting-room, a ladies' waiting-room, a restaurant, and other requisites for the accommodation of the great daily travel. North of the station, and extending to Arch Street, is the great train-shed of the company, two hundred and sixty-seven feet wide, and roofed by springing iron arches eighty-eight feet high in centre above the track-level. Here is ample space for thirteen tracks, eleven of which cross Arch Street on a bridgeway made of heavy iron girders, so treated with concrete and asphalt as greatly to deaden the sound of trains. The ground floor under the train-shed has been applied to

<small>Reading Terminal Station.</small>

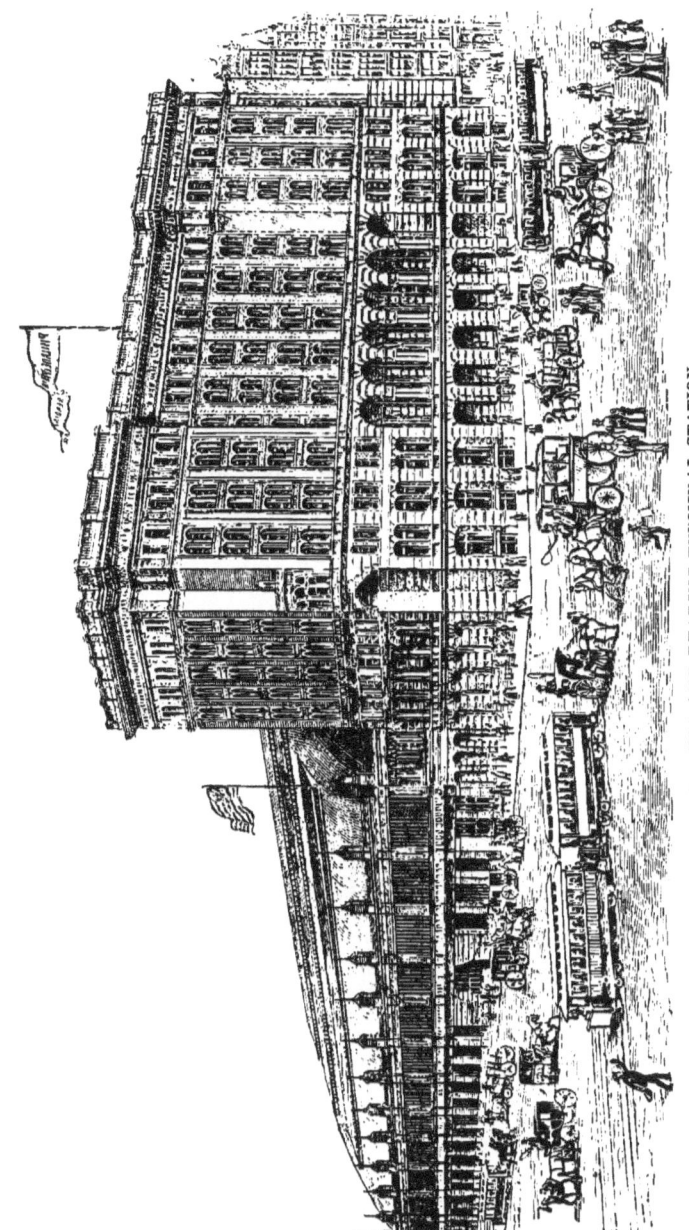

PHILADELPHIA AND READING TERMINAL STATION.

the use of the **Farmers' Market**, which formerly occupied the ground on which the station is built. This market, with its abundant space and complete equipment, its ample cold-storage vaults, its elevators running to the train-shed, and other advantages, is perhaps the best-appointed one now in existence, and is well worthy the attention of visitors to the city. The station here described connects with the new elevated track of the Reading Railroad, and replaces its former stations at Ninth and Green and at Broad and Callowhill Streets. North of Arch Street the road runs to Callowhill Street on a solid embankment enclosed by heavy stone walls, crossing the intermediate streets on arched stone bridges. At Callowhill Street it divides, one branch running to Broad and Callowhill Streets, where it reaches the level; the other to Ninth and Wallace Streets. From these points stretch out the ramifying lines of the Company, extending over a wide district north, east, and west. The new road and station are among the most important of the many recent improvements of Philadelphia, and are of invaluable service to the travelling public.

POST-OFFICE.

RECORD BUILDING.

II.

THE POST-OFFICE AND VICINITY.

FIVE squares east of the City Hall ("Public Buildings"), and fronting on Chestnut, Ninth, and Market Streets, stands the new

United States Post-Office.

United States government building, popularly known as the **Post-Office**, but in reality containing within its massive walls, besides perhaps the best appointed post-office in the country, the **United States Court-Rooms** and branch offices of the **Coast Survey**, the **Geological Survey**, the **Light-House Board**, the **Secret Service**, the **Signal Service**, and the offices of various officials of the Federal government. The building is of granite, four lofty stories in height, with a dome reaching one hundred and seventy feet above the level of the street, and has fronts of four hundred and eighty-four feet on Ninth Street and one hundred and seventy-five feet on Chestnut and Market Streets. The entrances to the public corridor are on the Ninth Street front, and the several departments of the post-office business are conveniently arranged on the first floor, extending from Chestnut to Market Streets, besides which, on this floor, the Western Union Telegraph Company has an office. Near each end of this corridor spacious stairways and hydraulic elevators lead to the upper stories. Ground was broken for the erection of this structure October 11, 1873, and the business of the post-office was first transacted within its walls March 24, 1884. Including the site, which cost the Government $1,491,200, about $8,000,000 were expended in its erection. Adjoining the post-office on Chestnut Street, and furnishing a striking architectural finish to that edifice, is the massive granite office of the **Philadelphia Record**, six stories in height, surmounted by a tower which rises to an altitude of one hundred and thirty-seven feet from the street pavement.

Adjoining the Record Building on the west is the stately new edifice of the **Penn Mutual Life Insurance Company**, perhaps the most attractive architectural adornment of this section of the city. This magnificent structure has a white marble front, rock-faced and tooled, seventy-

Penn Mutual Insurance.

PENN MUTUAL BUILDING.

seven feet wide, and one hundred and thirty-five feet (eight stories) high, while its tower, of attractive Saracenic architecture, is two hundred and five feet in height. A step farther westward may be seen the curious architecture of the **City Trust, Safe Deposit, and Surety Company's** building, with its front of dark marble and Indiana limestone. Still westward, at the north-west corner of Chestnut and Tenth Streets, stands the lofty and massive granite building of the **Mutual Life Insurance Company of New York**, one of the handsomest structures in the city.

City Trust and Safe Deposit Co.

Tenth Street, north and south of Chestnut, is the seat of a number of interesting institutions. At the corner of Sansom Street stands the well-known **Jefferson Medical College**, founded in 1826, and one of the most celebrated medical schools in this country; in the rear of which, on Sansom Street, is the **Jefferson Medical College Hospital**, a large edifice, with accommodations for one hundred and twenty-five patients. The College contains a highly valuable anatomical museum, which has recently been enriched by the extensive collection in morbid anatomy of the late Dr. S. D. Gross. This institution is about to be removed to new and more spacious quarters at Broad and Christian Streets, where it will have greatly increased facilities by the erection of ample college, hospital, and laboratory buildings. The new edifices are expected to be ready for occupancy in October, 1893.

Jefferson Medical College.

In this vicinity, at Nos. 911-915 Locust Street, is a charitable association worthy of notice,—the **Franklin Reformatory Home for Inebriates**, which was organized in 1872, and has done highly useful work in the purpose which its name indicates.

On Tenth Street, midway between Chestnut and Market, is the **Mercantile Library** building, an institution founded in 1820, and whose large collection of books and liberal measures for the accommodation of the reading public have long rendered it highly popular with our book-loving population. Formerly situated at Fifth and Library Streets, it was removed in 1869 to its present more ample building, where its stores have increased until it now possesses one hundred and sixty-six thousand volumes. The Mercantile has long been the people's library of Philadelphia. Its doors are open day and evening and during several hours on Sunday, its books are free to all readers, under proper regulations, and its members have immediate access to its shelves,—a valued privilege,

Mercantile Library.

MUTUAL LIFE INSURANCE BUILDING.

PHILADELPHIA COLLEGE OF PHARMACY.

in the granting of which the Mercantile was the pioneer among large libraries.

On North Tenth, above Arch Street (Nos. 139-145), is the new home, completed in 1892, of the **Philadelphia College of Pharmacy** This institution was organized in 1821, and is the oldest of its kind in the United States. The old college building on Filbert Street proved inadequate in 1867, and a new building was erected at 145 North Tenth. The latter has now been replaced by the present edifice, the largest in the world devoted solely to instruction in pharmacy. An important feature is the college museum, which contains the finest collection of medicinal plants in America, together with collections in materia medica, pharmaceutical and chemical apparatus and products. The instruction in this institution is largely practical, and embraces lectures and laboratory work in chemistry, pharmacy, materia medica, botany, and microscopy. Two large laboratories are open daily for instruction in analytical chemistry and operative pharmacy. There are nearly seven hundred students attending the various departments. Three thousand five hundred and sixty-five graduates are scattered throughout the American continent and Europe. The *American Journal of Pharmacy* has been published by the College since 1825.

<small>College of Pharmacy.</small>

On Cherry Street, just east of Eleventh, is the **First African Baptist Church**, and in this immediate vicinity, on the north side of Cherry, is the well-known **Aimwell School**, founded in 1796 by three young women, of the Society of Friends, and still supported by the **Society for the Free Instruction of Female Children**. At the south-west corner of Cherry and Eleventh Streets stands the new building of one of the most purely benevolent institutions of the city, **The Lying-In Charity**, established in 1828, for the assistance and care of deserving indigent women, both at their homes and in the wards of the Hospital. This institution is under the administration of distinguished physicians, and ladies of the city well known for their benevolence, and during its existence some fifteen thousand poor women have been cared for, and more than $175,000 dispensed for their benefit. The Charity also maintains a home and school for nurses, to whom instruction is given in the practical details of their calling. The new building was erected at a cost of over $50,000.

Somewhat north of this location, on Twelfth Street, above Race, is the building of the **Sunday Breakfast Association**, a society devoted to the amelioration of the condition of the poor and the reformation of inebriates. Removal to a new and better-adapted situation is contemplated.

On South Eleventh Street, at the corner of Clinton, is the new location of the **Pennsylvania College of Dental Surgery**, in the building recently occupied by the Oral Branch of the Deaf and Dumb Institution. This edifice is being greatly changed and adapted in all particulars to the needs of a dental college. The Pennsylvania College, chartered in 1865, is the direct successor of the Philadelphia College of Dental Surgery, organized in 1850. It has been since 1868 at Twelfth and Filbert Streets, but in its new building will have much better facilities for lectures and laboratory work.

{College of Dental Surgery}

At the north-west corner of Eleventh and Pine Streets stands the most striking example in Philadelphia of the apartment-house, now so common in our more crowded cities. This building, **The Gladstone**, is of ten stories in height and covers an ample ground-space, its appearance being very imposing. It is divided internally into numerous suites of apartments, each abundantly provided with conveniences. Nearly adjoining, at the south-west corner of Eleventh and Spruce Streets, is the **Colonial**, an apartment-house of smaller dimensions but of attractive exterior aspect and excellent interior arrangements. Other high-class examples of this order of edifices are the **Hotel Hamilton**, at 1334 Walnut Street, and the **Stenton**, at the north-east corner of Broad and Spruce Streets.

{Apartment-Houses}

Between the Gladstone and the Colonial apartment-houses, at 324 South Eleventh Street, stands the plain brick edifice of the **Lincoln Institution**, a useful charity, which was originally organized in 1866 as a school for soldiers' orphans, and in 1883 was transformed into a school for Indian girls, of whom it has accommodations for about one hundred. The course of instruction includes intellectual and industrial training. The school has a summer home near Wayne Station, on the Pennsylvania Railroad.

{Lincoln Institution}

In addition to the public institutions in the district surrounding the Post-Office, are to be seen a considerable number of the leading retail and wholesale stores of Philadelphia and several of the principal theatres, hotels, and newspaper-offices; the hotels including the **Continental, Girard House**, and **Bingham House**; the theatres, the **Chestnut Street Opera House, Chestnut Street Theatre**, and **Walnut Street Theatre**;

the newspaper-offices, the **Times, Press, Record, Inquirer,** and other buildings. Of the mercantile houses we can only name those which stand first in their class. On Market Street, extending from Eleventh to Twelfth, is a group of mammoth structures belonging to the Girard estate, chief among which is the immense establishment of **Hood, Foulkrod & Co.**, the largest wholesale dry-goods house of the city. Of the numerous large establishments on Chestnut Street, the one most interesting to visitors is the **Earle's Picture Galleries,** 816 Chestnut Street, whose collections are freely open to inspection and are much visited. In this connection it is proper to speak of the architecturally ornate **Haseltine Building** (1416–18 Chestnut Street), in which are a series of galleries of paintings and statuary, to which visitors are cordially welcome. Market Street from Eighth to Ninth contains a number of important mercantile establishments. Of these, that of **Strawbridge & Clothier** stands first, as the most extensive retail dry-goods house in the city and the rival of Wanamaker's in amount of business and diversity of goods. It occupies a building five stories in height, and extends from Market to Filbert Streets, with fronts of one hundred and fifty-five feet on Market and two hundred and thirty feet on Filbert Street. This house does an enormous retail business, including among its customers many of the wealthiest people of the city and its vicinity.

East of Eighth Street, at Nos. 715–17 Market Street, stands the widely-known book establishment of the **J. B. Lippincott Company,** one of the principal publishing houses of the United States, and the leading wholesale and retail book-store in the city.

J. B. Lippincott Company.

The edifice has a white marble front of some forty feet in width and five stories in height, and extends back three hundred and sixty-five feet to Filbert Street, on which it has a front of one hundred feet, and where it possesses a complete plant for the manufacture of the large number of volumes which this house annually issues. In addition to its publishing department, it has a large printing-office and bindery, and an extensive sale department of books, stationery of every description, and fancy goods.

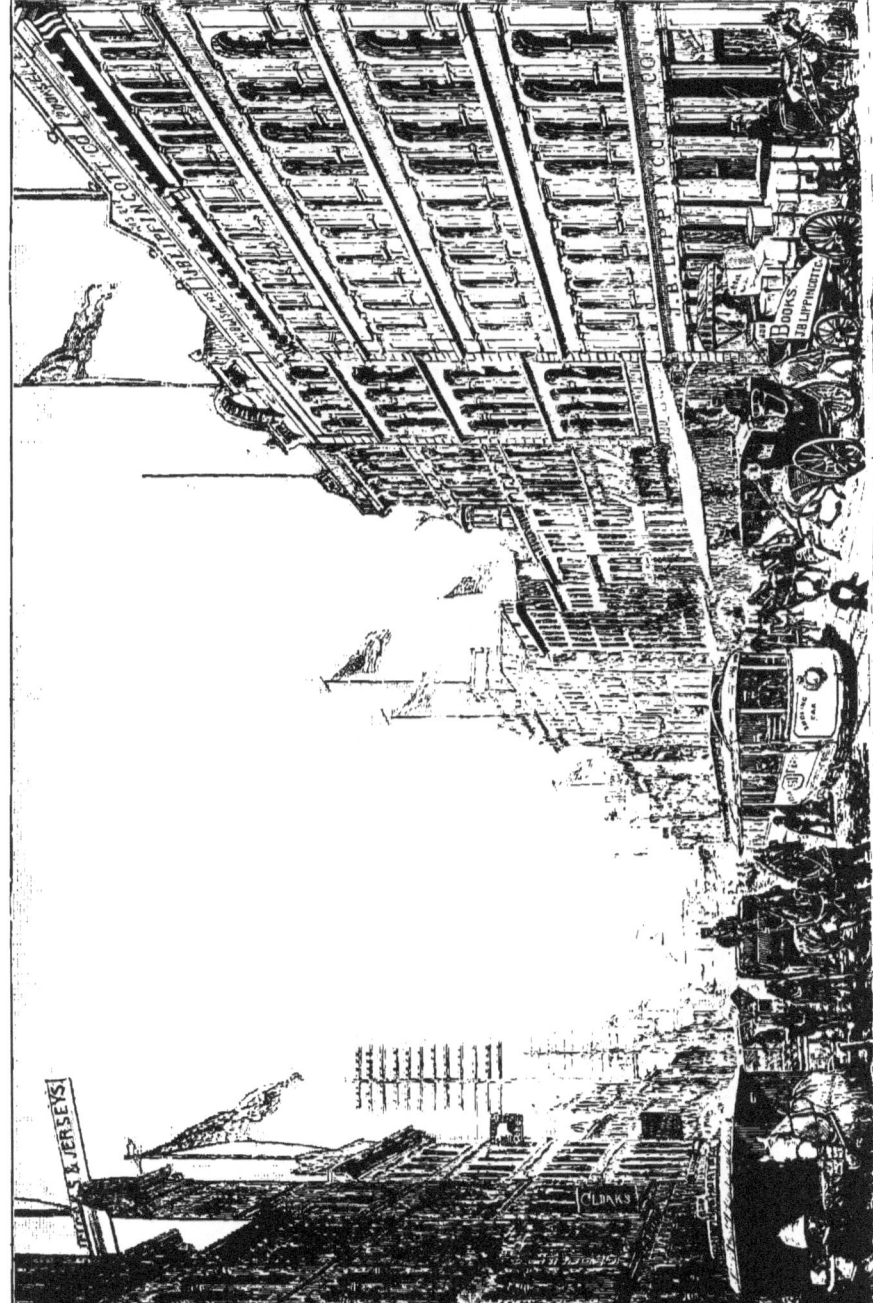

J. B. LIPPINCOTT COMPANY'S STORE.

III.

INDEPENDENCE HALL AND VICINITY.

EIGHT squares east of the new City Hall, on Chestnut Street between Fifth and Sixth Streets, stands the most famous of the old-time buildings of Philadelphia, the State House of colonial times, but since the Revolutionary War known as **Independence Hall**. Though built (1729–1735) by the Province of Pennsylvania for State purposes, the edifice is most intimately associated in the American mind with the year 1776 and the occurrences connected with the establishment of the United States government. Here in the principal hall—the east room on the first floor—was convened the Second Continental Congress, by whom it was resolved "That these united colonies are, and ought to be, free and independent States: and that all political connection between us and the State of Great Britain is, and ought to be, totally dissolved." In the same Hall also, in secret session, on July 4 of the same year (1776) Congress adopted the immortal Declaration of Independence, which on the 8th was publicly read to the assembled citizens in the State House yard, now known as Independence Square. In 1787 another event, of no less moment in American history, took place in this venerable Hall, that of the meeting of the memorable Constitutional Convention, and the drafting and adoption of the Constitution of the United States. The famous old bell, with its prophetic inscription, "Proclaim liberty unto the land, and to all the inhabitants thereof," is now preserved as a precious relic of the past in the museum of historical treasures which occupies one of the ground-floor rooms of the building. The other—that in which the Continental Congress sat—now contains the portraits of most of the members, with those of other heroes of the Revolution, the chairs in which these members sat, and other articles of historical interest. The old Hall is not only amply worth visiting in itself, but is destined long to continue a place of pilgrimage for all patriotic Americans.

Independence Hall.

Flanking Independence Hall on either hand and connected with it by a series of public offices (the whole known as "State House Row") are the *old* **City Hall**, at Fifth and Chestnut Streets,—long occupied as offices by the mayor and other city officials,—and the old **Congress Hall,** at Sixth and Chestnut Streets, which in the early days of the Republic was occupied by the different departments of the

INDEPENDENCE HALL.

Federal government. Here in the room of the House of Representatives, in the latter building, Washington, in 1793, was inaugurated president for the second time, and here John Adams, four years later, assumed the duties of the same office.

Adjoining the old City Hall, on Fifth Street below Chestnut, is the building of the **American Philosophical Society,** an outgrowth of the "Junto" Club, established by Dr. Franklin and others in 1743. This building, erected in 1787 upon ground donated to the Society by the Commonwealth, is occupied in part, under lease to the city, by some of the city courts, the upper rooms being reserved for the use of the Society, and containing its large library and other objects of interest. Among its presidents have been such notable men as Benjamin Franklin, David Rittenhouse, Thomas Jefferson, Stephen Duponceau, etc., and its membership has embraced many of the most notable citizens of Philadelphia. In its halls are read and discussed papers on philosophical and scientific subjects, which are published in its "Transactions" and "Proceedings," volumes which have a high standing in the world of science. The American Philosophical Society is much the oldest institution of its kind in America, while Europe possesses few of older date.

Philosophical Society.

In the rear of Independence Hall, extending to Walnut Street, is **Independence Square,** the scene of the first reading of the Declaration of Independence to the people. This took place on July 8, 1776, from the platform of an observatory erected in 1769 to observe the transit of Venus. Independence Square was long a favorite place for town-meeting assemblies and open-air public demonstrations. Here the citizens met to express their indignation against the Stamp Act, and in 1773 to insist that tea should not be unloaded at Philadelphia. In later years great political meetings were held here, and for many years the reading of the Declaration has been annually repeated here on Independence Day.

Independence Square.

Midway between Fifth and Sixth Streets, on the north side of Chestnut and fronting Independence Hall, is the new building of the **Pennsylvania Company for Insurances on Lives and Granting Annuities,** a thoroughly fire-proof structure extending from Chestnut to Minor Streets, a distance of two hundred and fifty-seven feet by eighty-one feet in width and one hundred feet high. Built in the Romanesque style of architecture, with an elaborately constructed granite front of massive proportions, this edifice presents a striking contrast to the buildings with which it is surrounded. The banking-room is one hundred and thirty-three feet long, seventy-seven feet wide, and fifty-two feet high, and is said to be the largest banking-room in the world, with

Pennsylvania Life & Trust Company.

PENNSYLVANIA COMPANY FOR INSURANCES ON LIVES AND GRANTING ANNUITIES.

perhaps a single exception. Organized in 1809, its prosperous career of more than three-quarters of a century has placed it in the very front rank of the institutions of its kind in the country, and vast interests—largely trusts and estates—are confided to its care.

Westward from Independence Hall may be seen several handsome bank buildings and other structures of much interest. At the corner of Sixth and Chestnut Streets is the extensive **Public Ledger** building, and adjoining it (Nos. 608-10) the attractive edifice of the **Land Title and Trust Company**, a building six stories in height, and fronting the street with a pair of grand windows that give it a striking architectural effectiveness. A square farther west, on the site of the old Masonic Temple, has been erected a massive and attractive stone block of banking-houses having the external appearance of a central building and two wings, but really consisting of three separate properties with a combined frontage of one hundred and ten feet and a depth of one hundred and seventy feet to Jayne Street. Here in the centre building (Nos. 715-717) is the new home of the **Union Trust Company**, adjoining which, on the west, is the **Chestnut Street National Bank**, the apartments of both being fitted up with great elegance.

On Seventh Street, above Chestnut, is located an institution of the highest public importance, the **Franklin Institute**, which was founded in 1824 for the promotion of the mechanic arts, and has ever since been a centre of active work in the instruction of the public. The building is a plain marble edifice containing a highly valuable scientific library and a much patronized lecture-room. A periodical, called the *Journal of the Franklin Institute*, in which are published many papers of high interest, has been issued since 1826. This Institute has given, in all, twenty-nine exhibitions of American manufactures, the pioneer of such exhibitions in the United States having been held at the old Carpenters' Hall in 1824. In addition, its annual courses of lectures, its drawing-schools, and its publications, have made it the foremost institution of its kind in this country.

Franklin Institute.

Opposite the Franklin Institute (Nos. 18-24 South Seventh Street) stands the edifice of the **Master Builders' Exchange**, an organization of builders and those connected with the building trades. The structure is three stories high in front and five in the rear, the whole first floor being occupied by the **Builders' Exchange Permanent Exhibition** of materials and objects used in the construction and finish of buildings. The

Master Builders' Exchange.

THE LAND TITLE AND TRUST COMPANY,
608 CHESTNUT STREET.

basement is usefully employed for the **Builders' Exchange Mechanical Trade Schools**, in which youths may obtain a valuable training preliminary to apprenticeship in the various building trades. These schools have been so successful as to attract wide-spread attention. On the second floor is an elegantly fitted-up exchange-room for the use of members, and on the third floor an excellent café for the accommodation of members and the general public. The remainder of the building is occupied by the various societies connected with the building trades. This institution is well worthy a visit.

At the south-west corner of Market and Seventh Streets is the site of the house in which Jefferson wrote the Declaration of Independence. This interesting historical edifice has vanished before the iconoclasm of trade, the **Penn National Bank** now occupying its site. Somewhat farther north (112 North Seventh Street) is an old-time charity,—the **Female Society for the Relief and Employment of the Poor**, usually known as "The House of Industry," which was organized in 1795, and has ever since been in active and useful operation.

South of Chestnut Street, at Nos. 606-14 Sansom Street, is an industrial establishment worthy of mention for its age and importance,—the type and electrotype works of the **MacKellar, Smiths & Jordan Company**, an industry established a century ago, and which has probably produced more printing material than any other concern in the country. It occupies part of the projected site of the new Mint, and will soon have to seek new quarters.

Of recent architectural achievements in Philadelphia none is more notable than the new edifice known as the **Philadelphia Bourse**, now in process of erection. This building occupies the whole space between Fourth and Fifth and Merchant and Ranstead Streets, with arcade approaches from Chestnut and Market Streets, the total structure being three hundred and sixty-two feet long by one hundred and thirty wide and ten stories in height. The first three stories are of stone, surmounted by light-colored brick to the tenth story, which is of ornate terra-cotta, the architectural effect of the combination being very pleasing. Interiorly, the first floor is occupied by the great hall of the Bourse, a room one hundred and twenty feet in width, divided by rows of columns into a broad centre fifty feet high and two side aisles each thirty-five feet high. This floor contains also several subsidiary rooms, and four large corner rooms adapted for banks or similar institutions. The upper floors to the ninth are designed to contain, in addition to ample exchange rooms for the use of individual mercantile exchanges, a large number of offices,—about seven hundred in all. The tenth floor is devoted to one of the leading purposes of the building,—that of a permanent museum of trade and industry. This great apartment, with a floor-space of nearly forty thousand square feet, fifteen feet in height, and abundantly lighted, is destined to prove an unceasing source of attraction to residents and visitors. The exhibition is continued in part of the basement, where arrangements for the display of machinery have been made. The cost of the building and ground is over $2,000,000. It is fire-proof throughout, and is one of the largest and most striking additions to the architectural adornments of Philadelphia that have been made for many years.

Quite without a rival among the business houses of the city, and equalled perhaps alone in point of magnificence by the new City Hall,

Drexel Building. the splendid **Drexel Building**, at Chestnut and Fifth Streets, towers high above all neighboring structures—a conspicuous object for miles around and affording from its roof a fine view of the city and surrounding country. Commenced in 1885, its germ was the new banking-house of Drexel & Co., erected in that year at the corner of Fifth and Chestnut Streets—itself an edifice that had few equals of its kind in the country. The completed structure, finished in 1888, extends over two hundred and twenty feet on Fifth Street by one hundred and forty-two feet on Chestnut Street (less the frontage of twenty-seven feet of the Independence National Bank), and covers a ground area of about thirty thousand square feet. Ten stories in height, the building rises one hundred and thirty-five feet above the street and contains over four hundred rooms, mostly occupied as offices by leading bankers and brokers, by corporations, lawyers, etc. The external walls of the building are faced with white marble, the body of the walls being of hard brick laid in Portland cement. Here on the first floor of the Chestnut Street front, at the corner of Custom House Place, is the **Tradesmen's National Bank**, over which, on the second floor, is the Board Room of the **Philadelphia Stock Exchange**, and above is the room of the **Philadelphia Board of Trade**. Nestled between the wings of the Drexel Building, at 430 Chestnut Street, its highly ornate front in striking contrast with the plain walls surrounding, stands the **Independence National Bank**.

The locality to which we have here introduced the reader is the site of a large number of financial institutions, many of them of high

DREXEL BUILDING.

interest for their architectural grandeur and beauty, and representing as a whole an amount of monetary business which is surpassed in few localities of like limited extent in the world. Of these numerous banks, insurance, trust, and other companies, we shall speak only of those whose extent, beauty of outward appearance, or history is likely to make them of interest to visitors. Several such institutions on Chestnut Street west of Fifth have already been mentioned. From Fourth to Fifth, on the north side of Chestnut Street, stands a group of structures whose appearance and importance demand some special notice. The new **Provident Building**, at the north-west corner of Chestnut and Fourth Streets, with its front of fifty-one feet on Chestnut Street by a depth of sixty-nine feet on Fourth, and an altitude of one hundred and fifty-two feet rising through ten stories, affords a striking example of a present tendency in architectural designs, and of a fashion in material now much in vogue. A room twenty-five feet in height adapted to banking purposes occupies the first floor, above which are about fifty offices, rendered easily accessible by rapid elevators. The exterior is composed of sections of a patent light brick and granite, arranged alternately with pleasing effect. This building is the property of the **Provident Life and Trust Company**, whose spacious offices occupy the massive granite edifice adjoining (Nos. 409-411 Chestnut Street), next to which (Nos. 413-417) is the building of the **Philadelphia Trust, Safe Deposit, and Insurance Company**. The solid granite building of the **Philadelphia National Bank** occupies Nos. 419-423, while the adjoining Nos. 425-429 are occupied by the graceful marble building of the **Farmers' and Mechanics' National Bank**, founded in 1807. At No. 435 is the **People's Bank**, a State institution.

[margin: Provident Building.]

On the south-west corner of Chestnut and Fourth Streets stands the solid **R. D. Wood Building**, of red brick with brown-stone trimmings, seven stories high, including the basement, and devoted to offices, to which access is had by swift elevators. Adjoining this is the plain marble building of the **Western National Bank**, next to which stands, in striking contrast, the United States Government Custom-House, originally erected (1819-1824) for the second United States Bank, the first having occupied the Girard Bank on Third Street below Chestnut. The Custom-House was modelled after the Parthenon at Athens, and is said to be one of the finest examples of the Doric order of architecture in the world. It is occupied by the Collector of

[margin: Government Custom-House.]

Customs and the Assistant Treasurer of the United States, with their respective assistants.

Eastward from Fourth Street on Chestnut are some splendid specimens of architecture in the banking-houses and other edifices with which the street is lined. At the south-east corner of Fourth and Chestnut is the stately banking-house of **Brown Brothers & Co.**, eight stories high, built of a peculiar light patent brick heavily trimmed with gray-stone, the first floor being devoted to the vast business of the firm and the upper rooms being occupied as offices by tenants.

UNITED STATES CUSTOM-HOUSE.

A few doors below, occupying Nos. 316-320 Chestnut Street, stands the massive building of the **Guarantee Trust and Safe Deposit Company of Philadelphia**, and nearly opposite (Nos. 327-331) is the beautiful marble edifice of the **Fidelity Insurance, Trust, and Safe Deposit Company.** The massive granite building of the **First National Bank** occupies Nos. 315-319, and adjoining it (No. 313) the building of the **National Bank of the Republic** attracts attention by its curious style of architecture,—presenting a striking façade of English red-stone and Philadelphia red pressed brick. Below the Bank of the Republic (No. 307)

GUARANTEE TRUST AND SAFE DEPOSIT CO., 316, 318, AND 320 CHESTNUT STREET.

NATIONAL BANK OF THE REPUBLIC, 313 CHESTNUT ST.

is the **Bank of North America**, the oldest bank in the country, its origin dating back to 1781. It occupies a plain, substantial structure, and may claim to be as substantial in its business record as in its appearance.

On Third Street, below Chestnut, are several financial institutions of interest. Among these we may particularly speak of the **Girard Bank**, a classical Grecian structure, whose marble portico faces the head of Dock Street. This building was erected for the first United States Bank, but when that institution went out of existence at the expiration of its twenty years' charter, it was purchased by Stephen Girard, and a bank established which became highly prosperous under his management. It sustained the government credit during the second war with Great Britain, and is still a prominent financial institution. On the opposite side of Third Street, between Walnut and Dock Streets, is the building known as the **Merchants' Exchange**, though it has long ceased to do duty as an exchange. The building is a handsome marble structure, having a semicircular front on Dock Street with a Corinthian portico. It was modelled after the choragic edifice at Athens known as the "Lantern of Demosthenes."

On Walnut Street, at the south-east corner of Third, is the edifice of the **Delaware Mutual Insurance Company**, adjoining which is the large building of the **Insurance Company of North America**. On the south-west corner of Third is the handsome building of the **Union Insurance Company**, adjoining which (No. 304) is the small but beautiful white marble Ionic structure of the **Royal Insurance Company**. Farther west (Nos. 331–337) stands the **Liverpool and London Globe Fire Insurance** building, and on the south-east corner of Fourth and Walnut Streets the massive and striking structure of the **American Life Insurance Company**. The rock-finished walls of this edifice, built of Wyoming Valley blue-stone, rise to the height of eight stories, and are surmounted by towers, the highest of which reaches a height of one hundred and sixty-five feet.

Westward on Walnut Street, midway between Fourth and Fifth, stands the building of the **Commercial Union Assurance Company of London**, eight stories in height, and built of buff brick with Indiana limestone trimmings. Another building of very attractive architecture on Walnut Street, west of Fourth Street, is that of the **Fire Association**, a white marble structure than which there are none more chaste and handsome in the city. Not far distant, at No. 136 South Fourth Street, is the building of the **Insurance Company of the State** of Pennsylvania, an institution organized in 1794, and, with one exception, the oldest of its kind in the United States. The edifice is seven stories in height, the front being richly ornamented with a copper oriel extending from the stone base to the sixth floor.

We have named but a portion of the financial institutions in the section under consideration, being obliged to confine ourselves to those of special architectural prominence. The same locality contains a number of other buildings of interest for their size or history, which may be disposed of briefly.

On the east side of Fourth Street, above Walnut, is the imposing Bullitt Building, built of brick, with heavy broken-stone columns and massive brown-stone trimmings. The walls of this enormous structure rise to a height of eight stories, and are surmounted by conspicuous towers on the Fourth Street front. The building contains the **Fourth National Bank**, the offices of several private bankers, and numerous other offices, with a popular restaurant on its upper floor.

Bullitt Building.

On Fourth Street, below Walnut, stand the main-office buildings of the **Pennsylvania Railroad Company** and the **Philadelphia and Reading Railroad Company**, large and massive structures, which will soon be in part or wholly superseded by the great buildings at the terminal stations of these two companies. In this vicinity are three churches of interest for their age and antique appearance. On the west side of Fourth Street, below the Pennsylvania Railroad building, is **St. Mary's Church** (Roman Catholic), a plain brick structure, which was erected in 1763; on Willing's Alley, in the rear of the Reading Railroad office, is **St. Joseph's**, another celebrated old-time Catholic church; and on Third Street, opposite Willing's Alley, is **St. Paul's Church** (Protestant Episcopal), which was built in 1761, but modernized in 1832.

With a reference to one more edifice, of the greatest historical interest, we may close this section of our subject. From the south side of Chestnut Street, midway between Third and Fourth, an open court yields a glimpse of a small and plain brick building which stands far back from the street. This is that famous edifice, the **Carpenters' Hall** of Revolutionary times, where, on September 5, 1774, assembled the first Continental Congress, and where, as an inscription on the wall proudly testifies, "Henry, Hancock, and Adams inspired the Delegates of the Colonies with Nerve and Sinew for the Toils of War;" the place where the

Carpenters' Hall.

BULLITT BUILDING.

first Continental Congress met, and where the famous "first prayer in Congress" was delivered by Parson Duché on the morning after the news of the bombardment of Boston had been received, and men knew that the war was indeed "inevitable."

Here the first Provincial Assembly held its sittings, to be succeeded by the British troops, and afterwards by the first United States Bank, and still later by the Bank of Pennsylvania.

Built in 1770, Carpenters' Hall was at first intended only for the uses of the Society of Carpenters, by whom it was founded. Its central location, however, caused it to be used for the meetings of delegates to the Continental Congress, and for other public purposes; and when no longer needed for these it passed from tenant to tenant, until it degenerated into an auction-room. Then the Company of Carpenters, taking patriotic counsel, resumed control of it, fitted it up to represent as nearly as might be its appearance in Revolutionary days, and now keeps it as a sacred relic. The walls are hung with interesting mementos of the times that tried men's souls. It is open to public visit and inspection, the entrance to the court being opened for visitors on business days, and is amply worthy the attention of patriotic citizens.

CARPENTERS' HALL.

IV.

Washington Square and Vicinity.

Washington Square, one of the five principal parks designated by William Penn as pleasure grounds for the inhabitants of his "great town," is a prettily laid out common of six acres, extending south and west from the corner of Sixth and Walnut Streets, adjoining Independence Square diagonally, and, like it, well-shaded with a variety of trees. Once a fashionable section of the city, it was in its early history surrounded by spacious residences, which are now principally devoted to lawyers' offices and kindred purposes, many of them having been remodelled or superseded by new buildings adapted to the changed condition of the locality. At the south-west corner of Walnut and Seventh Streets is located the massive granite building of the **Philadelphia Saving-Fund Society**, a benevolent institution, established in 1816, and now holding in trust for its depositors about thirteen millions of dollars. Opposite this institution, at 721 Walnut Street, is the building of the **Real Estate Investment Company of Philadelphia**, which exercises the functions of a real-estate broker and attorney. Fronting the Square, at the north-west corner of Seventh and Walnut Streets, are the rooms of the **Pennsylvania Bible Society**, established in 1808. On the east side of the Square, at the corner of Sixth and Adelphi Streets, is the brown-stone building of the **Athenæum Library and Reading-Room**, an institution organized for literary pursuits in 1814. In this building, in addition to the Athenæum library, is the **Law Association Library**, a valuable collection of legal works of reference. The **American Catholic Historical Society** also meets here. On the south side of the Square, at No. 614, is the new buff-brick building of the **Central News Company**, the leading mercantile concern for the distribution of periodical literature.

A half-square south of the Athenæum, at the north-west corner of Sixth and Spruce Streets, is the old Roman Catholic **Church of the Holy Trinity** (German), quaint in its exterior aspect, but not unattractive within. More than a century ago (1789) this church was dedicated to the use of the German Catholics. A small burying-ground is attached, and in its vaults the body of Stephen Girard once rested.

PHILADELPHIA SAVING FUND SOCIETY, SOUTHWEST CORNER OF SEVENTH AND WALNUT STREETS.

A parish school, known as the **Holy Trinity School**, is attached to this church, for which a substantial brick building, with a conspicuous tower, has lately been erected.

A square to the westward, at the south-west corner of Spruce and Seventh Streets, occupying a large building of brick, is **St. Joseph's Female Orphan Asylum**, conducted by the Sisters of Charity. This institution was established in 1807, for the reception of orphan girls of from four to seven years of age, of which some two thousand have since been furnished with homes gratuitously. They usually remain until about fourteen years of age.

Fronting Washington Square on the south, at the corner of Seventh Street, is the present edifice of the **First Presbyterian Church**, a society organized under the name of Independents, in 1698, and the first of that name formed in Pennsylvania. This building was erected in 1822, is of brick, rough-cast, having a front of seventy-five feet, with a fine portico, and a depth of one hundred and forty feet. It is noted as having been the scene of the pastoral labors of several distinguished clergymen, among the most celebrated of whom was the Rev. Albert Barnes, the eminent biblical scholar and theologian, who for nearly forty years ministered to this people. Near this church, at the south-west corner of Washington Square, is an entrance to the **Orange Street Friends' Meeting**, the principal entrance to which is, as its name implies, on Orange Street, above Seventh. At the south-east corner of Eighth and Locust Streets is the home of the **Penn Club**, an association of literary and professional gentlemen; and on Locust Street, above Eighth, is located **Musical Fund Hall**,—the property of the Musical Fund Society,—once one of the most fashionable concert-rooms in Philadelphia, and still considered second to none in the excellence of its acoustic properties.

Of other institutions in the vicinity of Washington Square, may be named the **Philadelphia Dispensary**, a charity now more than a century old, as it was established in 1786. The present building, No. 127 South Fifth Street, was erected in 1801. This useful institution is the oldest of its kind, not only in Philadelphia, but in the United States. Nearly twenty-five thousand patients were treated during the past year. On Seventh Street, at the corner of Sansom, is the **Union Benevolent Association**, which was organized in 1831, and has given relief to more than three hundred and fifty thousand persons, and distributed $1,000,000 in money and goods.

Of the institutions in the vicinity of Washington Square, however,

Pennsylvania Hospital. much the most important is the **Pennsylvania Hospital**, whose grounds and buildings occupy the entire area bounded by Spruce, Pine, Eighth, and Ninth Streets, and whose long career of usefulness entitles it to more than a passing notice.

In 1750 a number of benevolent persons applied to the Provincial Assembly for a charter for a hospital. The credit of originating the movement is due to Dr. Thomas Bond, at that time one of the most distinguished physicians of the city. Benjamin Franklin highly approved the project, and subsequently secured the charter, which was granted in 1751, in which year a few benevolent persons rented a private house, the residence of Judge John Kinsey, on the south side of Market Street, above Fifth, and there first established the hospital in 1752. In December, 1754, the square of ground, four and a quarter acres, except a portion which was given by the proprietors, Thomas and Richard Penn, was bought for five hundred pounds; this lot at that time was far out of town. On the 28th of May, 1755, the corner-stone of the present noble structure was laid, with the accompanying inscription prepared by Franklin. In December, 1756, patients were admitted, but it was not until 1800 that the hospital was finished according to the original plan.

"IN THE YEAR OF CHRIST
MDCCLV.
GEORGE THE SECOND HAPPILY REIGNING
(FOR HE SOUGHT THE HAPPINESS OF HIS PEOPLE),
PHILADELPHIA FLOURISHING
(FOR ITS INHABITANTS WERE PUBLIC-SPIRITED),
THIS BUILDING,
BY THE BOUNTY OF THE GOVERNMENT,
AND OF MANY PRIVATE PERSONS
WAS PIOUSLY FOUNDED
FOR THE RELIEF OF THE SICK AND MISERABLE.
MAY THE GOD OF MERCIES
BLESS THE UNDERTAKING."

Since the hospital was first opened nearly one hundred and seventeen thousand patients have been admitted within its walls. Its benefits have not been confined to the native-born. During the last ten years, of more than nineteen thousand admissions, only eight thousand five hundred were born in the United States. Medical and surgical cases are alike received, and any case of accidental injury, if brought within twenty-four hours, is received without question. This institution is, and always has been, the great "accident hospital" of this large and ever-increasing manufacturing city.

The first clinical lectures on medicine and surgery in America were given in this hospital, and these have been continued up to this present every Wednesday and Saturday morning.

The splendid medical library, containing nearly fifteen thousand volumes has been collected from the fees paid by the students for the privilege of attending these demonstrations.

The department for out-door relief assists annually many thousands of sick and injured poor. A large and valuable pathological museum also adds to the efficiency of the medical instruction.

There are eight attending surgeons and physicians, and four resident physicians, also a female superintendent of nurses (who graduate after a year's service), and an ambulance and telephone service.

The proper care of the insane was among the important objects sought to be accomplished by the establishment of the Pennsylvania Hospital. Until the year 1841 the insane were cared for in the parent hospital at Eighth and Pine Streets, but at this period they were removed to the hospital building which had been erected on the premises between Market Street and Haverford Avenue and Forty-second and Forty-ninth Streets.

V.

FRANKLIN SQUARE AND VICINITY.

FRANKLIN SQUARE, one of the five original parks dedicated to public use by William Penn, and named from its relative locality *North-East Square*, extends from Vine Street on the north to Race Street on the south, and from Sixth Street on the east to Franklin on the west, covering an area of over seven acres. It is well kept and finely shaded by large trees, and has a beautiful fountain in the centre.

Formerly the vicinity of Franklin Square was not without its claims as a desirable section for residences, of which there were many of the better class; but of late these have in great part given place to business-houses, generally of minor importance. Conspicuous among the present attractions of this locality is the handsome hall of the **Young Maennerchor** (at Sixth and Vine Streets), an association founded in 1852 and incorporated in 1869 "for the promotion of artistic taste in general and of vocal music in particular, by the practice and performance of sacred and secular music, and the establishment of a school for gratuitous instruction in singing and music." Seventy male and as many female voices constitute the

HALL OF THE YOUNG MAENNERCHOR.

present choral strength of this society, and among its trophies it numbers a first prize won in New York in 1852, second prizes won in New York in 1865 and in Baltimore in 1869, and a first prize won in the latter city in 1888.

The **Maennerchor Society**, an older musical association, founded in 1835, and long located at Fairmount Avenue and Franklin Street, has its head-quarters at 551-553 North Fifth Street. Its new building (now in process of erection) is a handsome and commodious edifice of buff Pompeian brick with gray Ohio-stone trimmings. It contains a fine concert-room, with seats for eight hundred people, a banquet-hall, restaurant, reception-hall, etc. The Maennerchor has five hundred and fifty members, and ranks high among the singing societies of America. Among its triumphs, it carried off first honors in the great musical contest at Newark, New Jersey, in 1891.

Maennerchor Society.

At 505 North Sixth Street is the plain brick building of the **Temporary Home Association**,—a useful charity, whose purpose is to provide a home at a very low rate of board for women temporarily out of employment. Children are also admitted. At No. 516 Race Street is the armory and hall of the **National Guards**, a military organization dating back to about 1835, and now known as the Second Regiment. It will soon remove from this locality to a new armory to be built on Broad Street north of Diamond Street.

Some distance north of Franklin Square, at the north-east corner of Spring Garden and Marshall Streets, stands the handsome new building of the **German Society of Pennsylvania**,—an ante-Revolutionary organization, it having been founded in 1764 for the relief of poor, sick, or distressed German immigrants. Formerly located on Seventh Street, in the building now used by the Builders' Exchange, it occupied its new quarters in 1887, the building being an attractive brown-stone and pressed-brick edifice, containing the assembly-hall and library of the Association. The latter, containing thirty thousand volumes, is considered the finest German library in the United States. Connected with the institution is a free employment bureau, through which some twelve hundred immigrants are supplied yearly with situations. Near this building, at the south-east corner of Spring Garden and Sixth Streets, is the fine granite building of the **Northern Saving-Fund, Safe Deposit, and Trust Company**, incorporated in 1871.

German Society Hall.

Farther west on Spring Garden Street, at the corner of Eighth, and extending to Green Street, is the plain four-storied brick building known as **Handel and Haydn Hall**,—deriving its name from a musical association of that title, though the building is principally occupied by stores and offices.

<small>Handel and Haydn Hall.</small>

Somewhat farther west, at Ninth and Green Streets, is the locality of the old Germantown Railroad Station, now superseded by the new

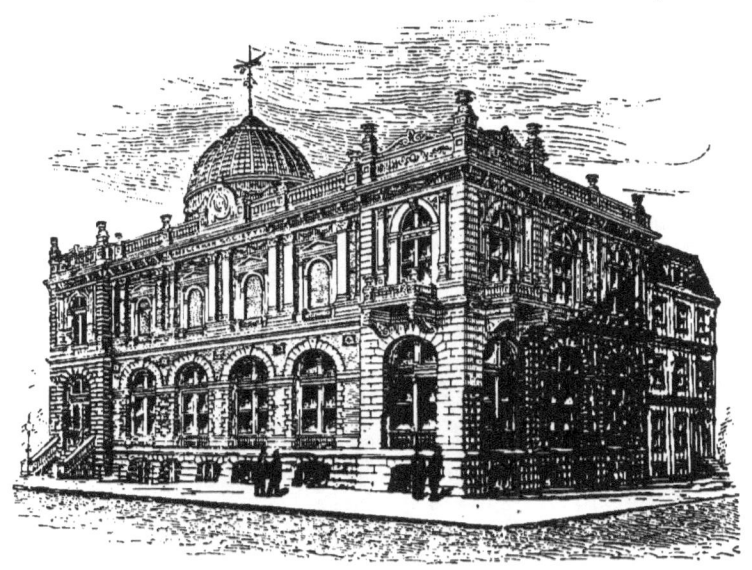

ASSEMBLY-HALL OF THE GERMAN SOCIETY OF PENNSYLVANIA.

Terminal Station; and near here, at Ninth and Parrish Streets, is one of those great industrial establishments which give such eminence to Philadelphia,—the **Powers & Weightman Chemical Works**, which, in connection with the extensive manufactory at Falls of Schuylkill, produce a line of fine chemicals and drugs for use in medicine and the arts perhaps unequalled by that of any other establishment in the country, and with few rivals in the world.

<small>Powers & Weightman Chemical Works.</small>

At the south-west corner of Arch and Fifth Streets is located, in the old meeting-house of the Free Quakers (the "Fighting Quakers" of the Revolution), the **Apprentices' Library**, established in 1820, "for the use of apprentices and other young persons, without charge of any kind for the use of books," and now containing a free reading-room and a library of from twenty-five to thirty thousand volumes, selected with special care for boys and girls. On the opposite side of Fifth Street from this library, in Christ Church burying-ground, and very near the corner of Fifth and Arch Streets (as may be seen recorded upon a flat stone, through a palisade railing set in the brick wall), lie the remains of Benjamin Franklin and his wife Deborah. Many other distinguished citizens lie buried in this ground, the resting-places of some of whom are marked by monuments. The vicinity of Franklin Square, in other directions, possesses few attractions beyond the stately business-houses that have lately been erected, both on Arch Street and on some of the cross-streets. At Arch and Sixth Streets are several lofty structures of comparatively recent erection, while from Seventh Street westward on Arch are a number of other large mercantile houses. In the vicinity of the Square are also a large number of industrial and manufacturing establishments. Of these we shall speak only of the **William H. Horstmann** manufactory and warehouse, situated at the corner of Fifth and Cherry Streets, perhaps the largest establishment in the country for the production of military and society goods.

Apprentices' Library.

FRANKLIN'S GRAVE.

The most interesting institution in this locality is the **Arch Street Meeting** of the Society of Friends, the oldest religious establishment

Arch Street Friends' Meeting. in the city, with the exception of the Old Swedes' Church. It is situated at Fourth and Arch Streets, occupying a lot, the gift of William Penn, of three hundred and sixty by three hundred and sixty-six feet in area, the building itself being about two hundred feet front. This ground was for a century and a half used as a graveyard; many thousands of bodies are buried here, interments having continued until about 1840. The Society met at Second and Market Streets until 1804, when the present building was erected. At present it is but little used, few Friends residing in the vicinity. There are services every Thursday, and the Yearly Meeting of the Society is held here.

VI.

RITTENHOUSE SQUARE AND VICINITY.

Rittenhouse Square. RITTENHOUSE SQUARE, a well-kept and finely-shaded common of six acres, the "South-west Square" of Penn's time, and called by the latter name from its relative position to the "Centre Square" of those days, where now stands the new City Hall, extends from Walnut Street south to Locust, and from Eighteenth Street to Nineteenth, its immediate surroundings embracing the most fashionable section of the city. Here almost unbroken blocks of costly mansions attest the vast wealth of those who are so fortunate as to be reckoned among the residents of that locality, while numerous churches (some of them of much elegance) erected here and there, on eligible sites, add not a little to the attractiveness of the section. A growing lack of uniformity in the style of architecture and of the material both of the private residences and of the public edifices gives variety to the scene. Here and there may be seen massive brick and brown-stone mansions of impressive sombreness and solidity, while not unfrequently, in the immediate neighborhood of buildings of this style, will be found a fancy patent-brick structure or a modern light-stone front.

Holy Trinity P.E. Church. Fronting the Square, at the corner of Nineteenth and Walnut Streets, stands the well-known and popular **Church of the Holy Trinity** (Protestant Episcopal), a Gothic structure of brown-stone, handsomely furnished, with a tower one hundred and fifty feet high. This church, first opened for worship in 1859, is a fine specimen of the most approved style of architecture of three decades ago, and its several rectors since have been men eminent in their profession. In the rear, on Twentieth Street, is the **Holy Trinity Parish House**, a commodious and handsome buff-brick edifice.

Academy of Notre Dame. Three doors from the Church of the Holy Trinity (at No. 206 South Nineteenth Street), and fronting on the Square, is the Roman Catholic **Academy of the Sisters of Notre Dame**, a substantial structure of brick with brownstone trimmings.

Fronting Rittenhouse Square on the east is the attractive mansion

RITTENHOUSE SQUARE.

of the late Joseph Harrison, noted for his career as a civil engineer and constructor of railroads, in which occupation, under contracts with the Emperor of Russia, he amassed a large fortune; and on Walnut Street, above Eighteenth (No. 1811), is the home of the **Rittenhouse Club**, a social, non-political organization possessing the general characteristics of the old Philadelphia Club, of which it may be considered the offspring. At the northeast corner of Chestnut and Eighteenth Streets is the **Philadelphia City Institute**, founded in 1852, in which is maintained a free public library, open afternoon and evening, where, in addition to accommodations for visitors, books are loaned under certain regulations. The volumes in the library number about fourteen thousand five hundred, and the number of visitors has increased within a few years from thirty thousand to one hundred and twenty thousand per annum.

Rittenhouse Club.

City Institute.

On the south side of Chestnut Street, west of Nineteenth (No. 1910), stands the **Aldine Hotel**, its main part occupying the former residence of Mrs. Rush (the widow of Dr. James Rush), in her day a leader of Philadelphia society, and to the generosity of whose husband the city owes its magnificent Ridgway Library. The hotel opens upon pleasant gardens in the rear, and is noted as a *family house*.

Aldine Hotel.

Two squares west of the Aldine Hotel, on Chestnut Street, a group of fashionable churches attracts the attention of the observer. Midway between Twenty-first and Twenty-second Streets, on the south side of Chestnut, stands **St. Paul's Reformed Episcopal Church**, the leading church of that denomination in Philadelphia, and having for its rector the bishop of the diocese. Nearly opposite, on the north side of Chestnut, is the beautiful edifice of the **First Unitarian Church**, whose congregation, organized near the close of the last century, formerly had their home at Tenth and Locust Streets, where for more than half a century they were ministered to by the Rev. Dr. William H. Furness. Adjoining this church, at the corner of Chestnut and Twenty-second Streets, is the **New Jerusalem Church** (Swedenborgian), one of the architectural ornaments of Philadelphia, having connected with it an auxiliary building containing Sunday-school rooms, a ladies' parlor, free library and reading-room, and a room devoted to the sale and distribution of books and tracts. These

St. Paul's Reformed Episcopal Church.

Unitarian Church.

Swedenborgian Church.

ALDINE HOTEL.

FIRST NEW JERUSALEM (SWEDENBORGIAN) CHURCH.

buildings are of the Gothic order of architecture, the church edifice representing the early English Gothic of the thirteenth century, and the auxiliary building the Gothic of a later period.

At Twenty-fourth and Chestnut Streets, on the Schuylkill River where it is spanned by the Chestnut Street bridge, stands the passenger station of the **Baltimore and Ohio Railroad**, an attractive brick structure with brown-stone trimmings, in the Queen Anne style of architecture. It has spacious apartments, consisting of restaurants and separate waiting-rooms for ladies and gentlemen, on the level of Chestnut Street, whence broad descending stairways (with walls of glazed tiles) and elevators lead to the ticket-offices on the first floor, thirty feet below,—level with the tracks, and with Twenty-fourth Street. The station has a front of one hundred and sixty feet on Chestnut Street by a depth of one hundred and thirty-five feet, its general height being fifty-five feet above the street, with a tower finial over one hundred feet high. The train-shed connected with the station is three hundred feet long by one hundred and ten feet wide, and is lit throughout by electricity. Through a close business connection between the Baltimore and Ohio and the Philadelphia and Reading Railroads, passengers for New York and for intermediate points may embark at this station, and passengers from New York, by the same trains, may land here.

Balt. & Ohio R.R.Station.

On Twenty-first Street, below Market, is the **Armory of the First Troop Philadelphia City Cavalry**, the oldest cavalry company in the country, and the oldest military association organized (November, 1774) for the special purpose of resistance to Great Britain. The building has an effective appearance, resembling, with its square tower and gateway and loopholed windows, a Middle Age fortress. The exercising room is one hundred and fifty feet long and over sixty feet wide, giving ample opportunity for cavalry exercises.

First Troop Philadelphia Cavalry.

On Twenty-second Street, below Walnut, is the **Children's Hospital of Philadelphia**, a plain brick structure in which children under twelve years of age are received for treatment. The Hospital has eighty-seven beds, and an average of about sixty children under treatment. A country branch, for convalescent children, has been established west of George's Hill in the Park, with excellent results.

Children's Hospital.

Farther south, at the north-east corner of Twenty-second and

BALTIMORE AND OHIO RAILROAD DEPOT, TWENTY-FOURTH AND CHESTNUT STREETS.

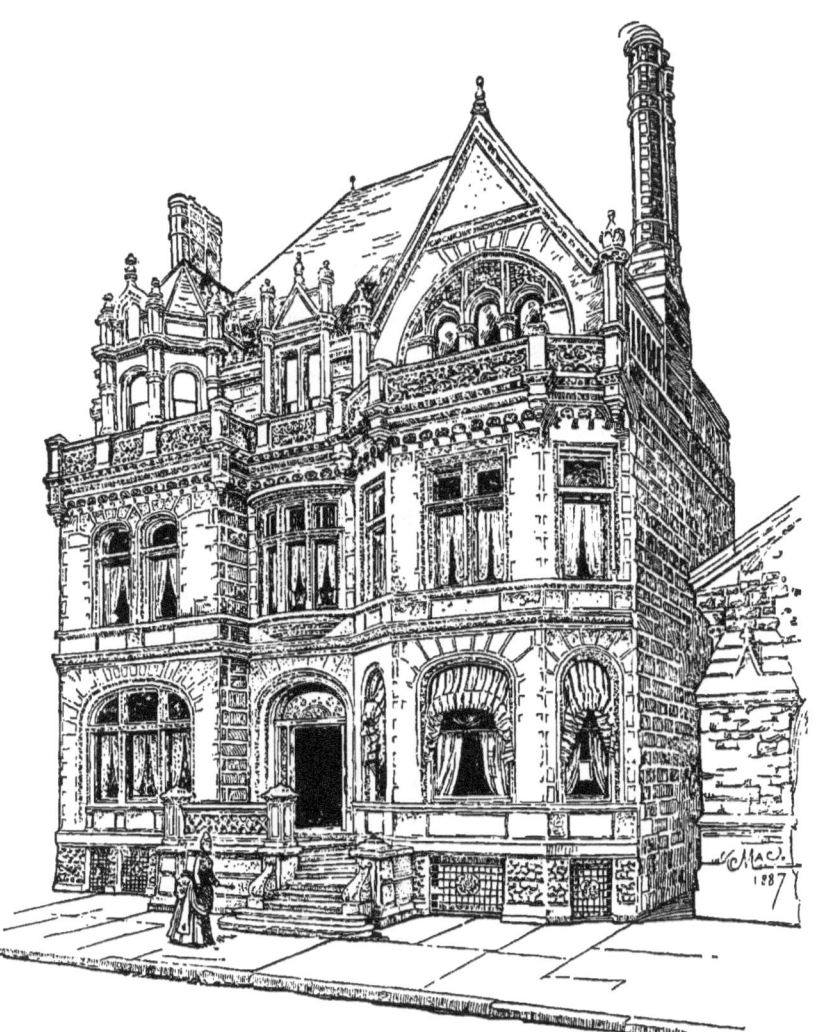

RESIDENCE ON WEST WALNUT STREET.

Pine Streets, is another of Philadelphia's useful institutions for the care of the sick, the **Rush Hospital for Consumptives**. Diseases of the throat and chest, and allied disorders, are also treated. This Hospital was opened for in-door patients in 1892. It has ten beds and a staff of four physicians.

Rush Hospital.

At some distance south of the Square, on Lombard Street west of Eighteenth, is the spacious new building of the **Philadelphia Polyclinic and College for Graduates in Medicine**. This institution, formerly at Broad and Lombard Streets, occupied its new edifice in 1891. It is a four-story structure, built of sandstone, brick, and terra-cotta, and contains several clinic rooms, a lecture-hall, chemical, physiological, and microscopical laboratories, etc. Connected with it is a training-school for nurses. The great variety of diseases treated here make it an excellent school of experience for medical graduates.

Philadelphia Polyclinic.

CATHEDRAL.

VII.

LOGAN SQUARE AND VICINITY.

LOGAN SQUARE, the north-west of the five principal parks reserved by William Penn for public use, and hence formerly called *North-West Square*, is a beautiful plot of seven and three-fourths acres, a half mile north-west from the City Hall, and occupying the square extending from Race Street on the south to Vine Street on the north, and east and west from Eighteenth to Nineteenth Streets. Besides the cars on these several streets which pass the square, this locality is reached by the cars on both Arch and Callowhill Streets, which run both east and west, by the cars on Seventeenth and Twentieth Streets from the northern section of the city, and by the Market Street cars, which pass two squares away. The immediate surroundings of Logan Square are mostly dwellings of a superior character, interspersed with various institutions, the striking feature of the locality being,

| Roman Catholic Cathedral. | *par excellence*, the Roman Catholic **Cathedral of St. Peter and St. Paul**, on Eighteenth Street above Race, a fine brown-stone edifice with a front on the street of one hundred and thirty-six feet, consisting of a |

portico of four massive pillars sixty feet high, supporting a pediment which reaches one hundred and one feet six inches above the street. This building has an external depth of two hundred and sixteen feet, is surmounted by a dome fifty-one feet in diameter, and has an extreme height of two hundred and ten feet. In the interior the building is cruciform, the nave being fifty-one feet wide by one hundred and eighty-two long, and the transepts fifty feet wide by one hundred and twenty-eight in length. The walls and vaulted ceilings (the latter eighty feet high) are richly decorated with Bible scenes,—over the grand altar being a striking painting of the crucifixion, by Brumidi. The corner-stone of this building was laid in 1846, and in 1864 the structure was dedicated with imposing ceremonies. Flanking the Cathedral on the one hand (at Eighteenth and Race Streets) is the Cathedral School for boys, and on the other, at Eighteenth and Summer Streets, is the archiepiscopal residence. Other institutions in the immediate neighborhood belonging to the same denomination are the **Catholic Home for Destitute Children**, on Race Street east of Eighteenth, and that estimable charity, **St. Vincent's Home**, for destitute infants and little children, at Eighteenth and Wood Streets. At No. 1815 Arch Street is the attractive brown-stone, rock-finished building of the **Academy of the Sacred Heart**, a flourishing Catholic institution.

At the corner of Nineteenth and Race Streets stands one of the most widely-known institutions of the city, the **Academy of Natural Sciences of Philadelphia**. This society, the oldest of its kind in America, began its career in 1812, successively occupying several locations until, in 1876, it removed to its present edifice. The building is a massive Gothic structure in green serpentine, adjoining which is a neat lecture-hall, in which courses of popular scientific lectures are annually given. The museum having proved inadequate to display the extensive collections of the Academy, there has recently been added a large wing, with a front of one hundred feet on Nineteenth Street, a depth in part of one hundred and thirty feet, and five stories in height. A second wing, fifty by one hundred and thirty feet, on Cherry Street, is projected. These additions will give immense museum space, and aid the Academy to sustain the reputation which it has long held,—that of being the foremost scientific institution in this country. The natural history materials of the museum are enormous in every field of biology. The collection of birds was until within the past twenty years unequalled by that of any museum in Europe. The collection of shells has nowhere, except in the British Museum, a rival in scientific value and completeness, while its recent addition of the shells of the United States, fossil and recent, made by the American Conchological Association, is unique and invaluable. Each of the other branches of biology is abundantly represented, while the scientific material collected by the Pennsylvania State Geological Survey, and here deposited, is of the highest interest and value. Another feature of importance is the bacteriological laboratory, which is one of the best equipped in this country. The library contains over thirty thousand volumes, numbers of them being superbly illustrated works. It is considered the most complete library of natural history in the United States. The Academy has long been prominent in scientific movements, the most recent of which was the eminently successful Peary Greenland expedition, sent out under its auspices, and which has added to its museum a magnificent collec-

WOMEN'S CHRISTIAN ASSOCIATION.

SCHUYLKILL NAVY ATHLETIC CLUB, 1626-28 ARCH STREET.

tion of the biological and ethnological treasures of Greenland. No visitor to the city should fail to see this admirable institution.

On the south-west corner of Eighteenth and Arch Streets stands the handsome and spacious new building of the **Women's Christian Association**, one of the leading architectural features of this section of the city. Covering an extensive ground space, and nine stories in height, it affords ample opportunities for the useful work of this society, which has for its object "the temporal, moral, and religious welfare of women, especially young women who are dependent upon their own exertions for support." The building, which has a granite base and buff brick superstructure, contains an employment office, an industrial school, a restaurant, library, and other advantages for the young women who find a home here at low rates of board. The Association maintains a college at Asbury Park for the benefit of its boarders, and is in charge of the "Whelen Home for Girls," at Bristol, Pennsylvania, designed as a temporary summer home for working girls.

Women's Christian Association.

East of this locality, on the south side of Arch Street, midway between Sixteenth and Seventeenth Streets, is the imposing building of the **Schuylkill Navy Athletic Club**, one of the handsomest and best-equipped club-houses in the city. This building, constructed from designs by Willis G. Hale, is five stories high, with a front of forty-five feet, and a depth of one hundred and forty-five feet, is built of Indiana limestone, with a granite base, and is surmounted by a mansard roof of Spanish tiles, having a tower finial reaching one hundred and nineteen feet above the pavement. Its apartments include, besides the parlor and reading-room, a main hall thirty-two by forty-two feet in extent, bowling-alleys, swimming-pool, barber-shop, a large billiard-room, lavatories, etc. A gymnasium forty-two by one hundred and forty-three feet, and a running-track, are on the upper floors. On the fifth floor is a racquet court and a summer pavilion forty-five by sixty-five feet, covered with canvas. The house is said to be one of the most perfect of its kind in the country.

Fronting Logan Square on the south, at No. 1810 Race Street, are the attractive building and grounds of the **Wills Eye Hospital**, the outcome of a bequest to the city by James Wills, who died in 1825, leaving a legacy for the erection of a free hospital for the treatment of diseases of the eye. This institution has a corps of ten eminent specialists, with as many assistant surgeons, and is of the greatest utility, there having been treated

Wills Eye Hospital.

here during the past year twelve thousand two hundred and eighty patients, while two thousand seven hundred and sixty-three operations were performed.

In the immediate neighborhood of the Cathedral, at the corner of Seventeenth and Summer Streets, stands the **Philadelphia Orthopædic Hospital and Infirmary for Nervous Diseases**, first estab-

Orthopædic Hospital.

lished in 1867, as the Philadelphia Orthopædic Hospital, for the treatment of club-foot, spinal and hip diseases, and other bodily deformities, its scope being afterwards (in 1870) enlarged so as to include the treatment of nervous diseases. Subsequently (in 1886) the original hospital buildings were torn down, and the present edifice was erected, combining all that art and science, ingenuity and experience could suggest in securing the best hospital accommodation. The visitor will be amply repaid for whatever time he can devote to a tour through the buildings.

At a short distance south of this locality, on Cherry Street, west of Seventeenth Street, is situated the **Medico-Chirurgical College and Hospital**, consisting of college and laboratory buildings,

Medico-Chirurgical College and Hospital.

and an attractive hospital building, of brick and rock-faced stone. This association has been in existence twelve years, and lays claim to a high standard of medical education, the faculty consisting of eleven professors and a corps of thirty instructors. The hospital contains one hundred and fifty beds. Occupying the eastward section of this large group of buildings is the **Philadelphia Dental College**, an

Philadelphia Dental College.

institution chartered in 1863, and formerly located at No. 108 North Tenth Street. It is a flourishing college, with a large number of students. Operations are performed in Oral Surgery in connection with the Medico-Chirurgical Hospital, with which this College is closely affiliated.

Westward from Logan Square, at Race and Twentieth Streets, is the **Pennsylvania Institution for the Instruction of the Blind**, which was

Blind Asylum.

founded in 1833, and has since pursued a highly useful career. It occupies spacious grounds and buildings, in which the inmates are instructed in the plain branches of an English education and in music, and are taught several industries. Adjoining the Blind Asylum, on Twenty-first Street, with grounds extending from Race to Summer Streets, is the four-story building of the **Asylum of the Magdalen Society**, an institution founded about 1800 for the reclamation of fallen women. It has room for

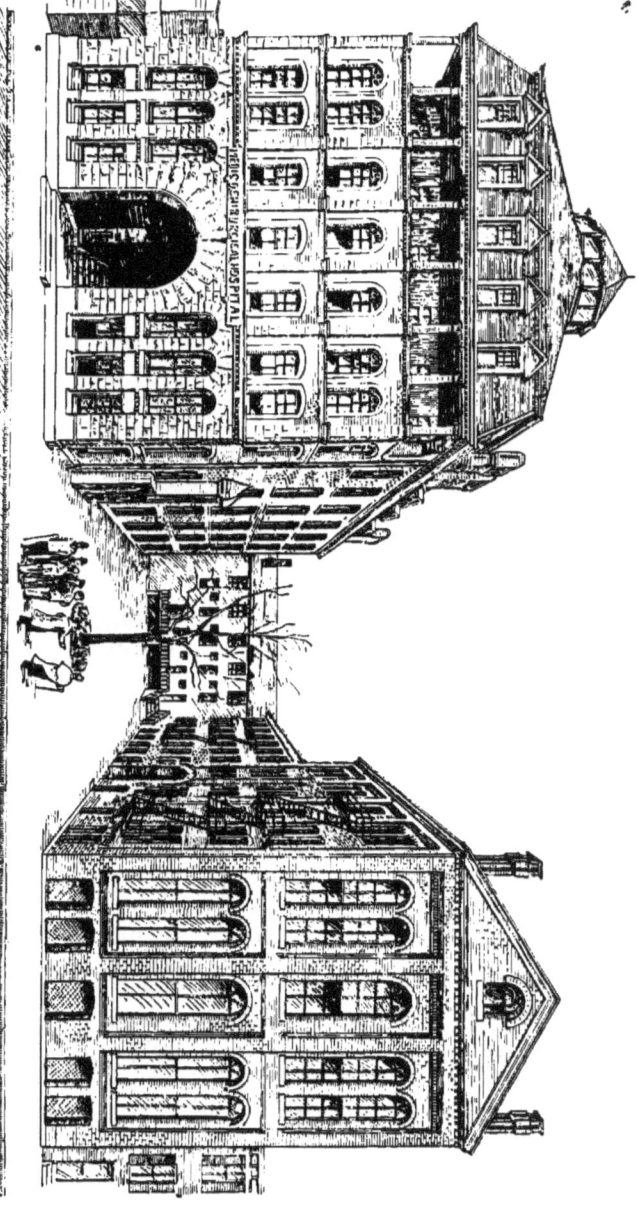

BUILDINGS OF THE MEDICO-CHIRURGICAL AND PHILADELPHIA DENTAL COLLEGES, AND THE CONJOINED HOSPITAL.

thirty inmates. A similar institution, the **Asylum of the Rosine Association**, situated at No. 3216 Germantown Avenue, has accommodations for about the same number of inmates.

At some distance north of Logan Square, on Hamilton Street, occupying the space between Twentieth and Twenty-first Streets, are the ample grounds of another of the many admirable charitable institutions in this vicinity, the **Preston Retreat**. Its origin is due to a legacy left by Dr. Jonas Preston, in 1836, to build and endow a lying-in home for poor married women. The institution possesses a handsome white marble building, with a stately Doric portico, surrounded by well-shaded and attractive grounds. It has accommodations for about thirty inmates.

An important projected improvement to the section under consideration is a broad and handsome **Boulevard**, to run diagonally from the City Hall to Fairmount Reservoir, with a width of one hundred and sixty feet, bordered by dwellings of the highest order of architectural beauty. This Boulevard will cross Logan Square, and will afford a direct approach from the centre of the city to Fairmount Park. It cannot fail to prove a highly-attractive addition to the city.

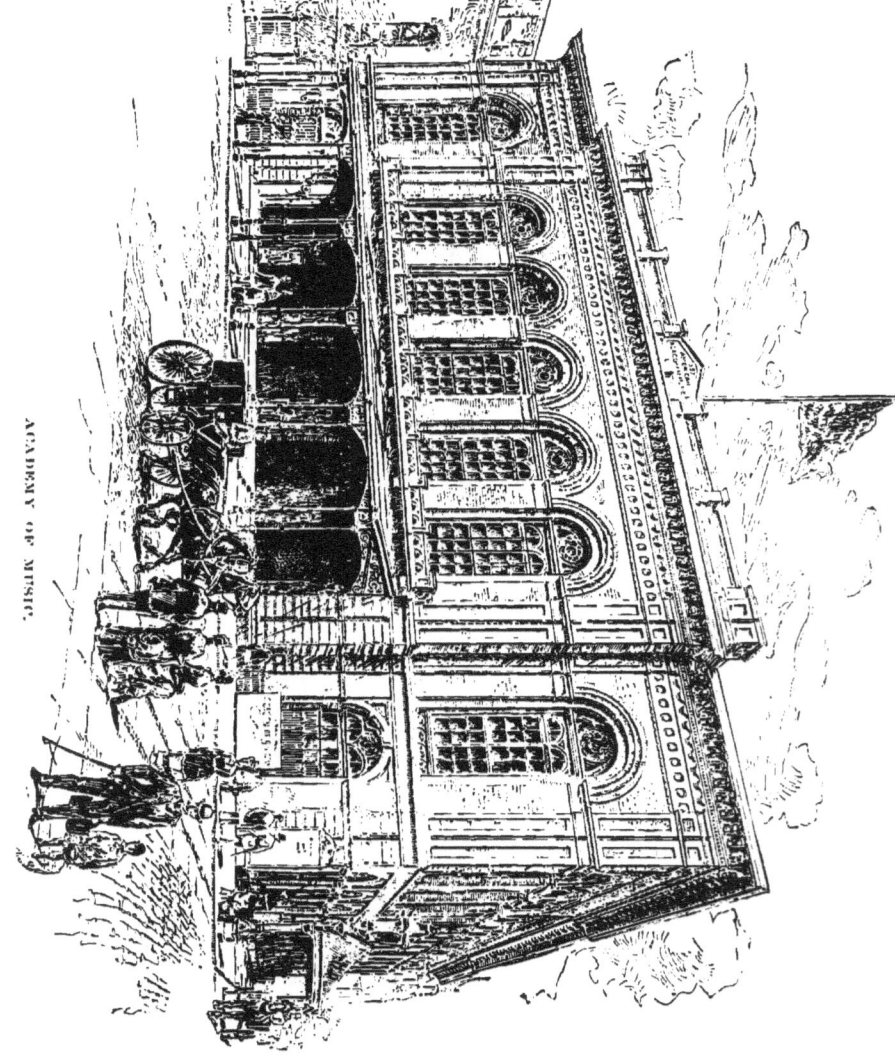

ACADEMY OF MUSIC.

VIII.

Broad and Locust Streets and Vicinity.

THE vicinity of Broad and Locust Streets, famous as the site of numerous institutions of note, is easily reached by street-cars from almost all sections of the city; from the extreme northern and southern parts by the cars of the Thirteenth and Fifteenth Streets line, from the east by the cars up Walnut or Pine Street, from Fairmount or the south-west (Gray's Ferry) by the Spruce and Pine Streets line, and from West Philadelphia by the various lines that converge and run eastward on Chestnut or Market Street. Situated at the southwest corner of Broad and Locust Streets is the **American Academy of Music**, erected in 1856 and held to be intrinsically the finest music-hall in America. **Academy of Music.** It is capable of seating two thousand nine hundred persons, and has a stage ninety feet wide by seventy-two and one-half feet deep, affording abundant room for the production of operatic and dramatic representations. Its superior acoustic properties make it a favorite both with actors and audiences, and here the brightest stars of the stage are wont to delight assemblies which, in point of numbers, culture, and fashion, compare favorably with like gatherings in any other part of the world. A few doors above the Academy (No. 220 South Broad Street) is the beautiful building of the **Art Club of Philadelphia**, of Pompeian brick and elaborately carved Indiana lime-stone, having a main front on Broad Street of sixty-four feet, with an overhanging **Philadelphia Art Club.** loggia of stone, and a side-front on Brighton Street of one hundred and sixteen feet, and claimed to be the only specimen of pure Renaissance architecture in Philadelphia. A picture-gallery, forty by sixty-four feet, devoted to the exhibition of paintings, with a beautifully decorated mantel of English red-stone and wood-work of cherry, is located upon the second floor, besides which the building contains a smaller exhibition gallery for water-colors and minor works of art, a café and restaurant, a reception-room and parlors common to all the members of the club, and a reception-room and restaurant for the exclusive use of ladies belonging to the families of members. In the picture-gallery are annually given several exhibitions of high interest to lovers of the fine arts.

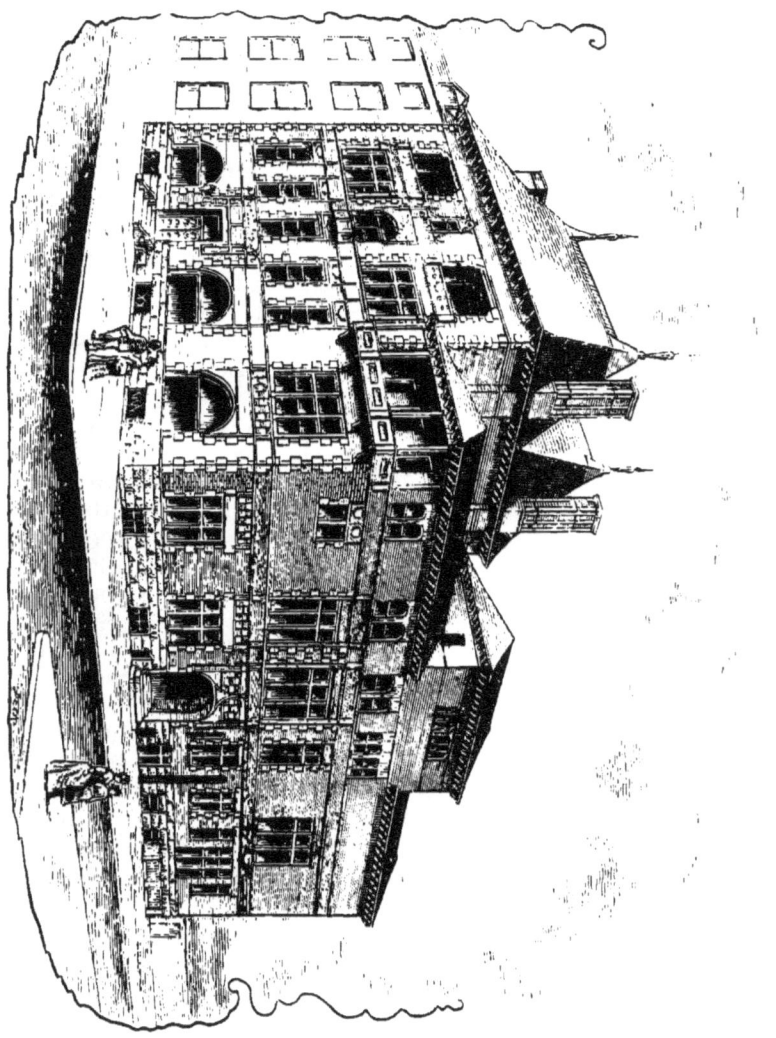

PHILADELPHIA ART CLUB.

Opposite the Academy of Music are two of the newer places of amusement of the city,—the **Empire** and the **Broad Street Theatres**,— and adjoining it, on the south, stands **Horticultural Hall**, the building of the Pennsylvania Horticultural Society, an institution founded in 1827, and, like so many other Philadelphia enterprises, the first of its kind in this country.

Horticultural Hall.

The Hall is periodically used for exhibitions of the floral triumphs of the amateur and professional horticulturists of the city and its vicinity, which are shown here to excellent advantage, and are a source of great interest to lovers of flowers.

Locust Street, east of Broad, is the seat of some old and notable institutions. At 1324 Locust Street is the **Episcopal Academy** (the "Academy of the Protestant Episcopal Church in the city of Philadelphia"), one of the leading preparatory schools of the city. Founded in 1785, and chartered by the Legislature of the Commonwealth in 1787, it has had over a century of active and useful existence.

At the north-west corner of Locust and Juniper Streets stands the main building of the **Philadelphia Library Company,** which was founded in 1731 by Benjamin Franklin and his associates of the "Junto" Club. This—the first subscription library established in America—was originally located near Second and Market Streets, afterwards received temporary quarters in the State House and Carpenters' Hall, until, eventually, in 1789, a building was erected for it on Fifth Street below Chestnut, on a lot now covered by the Drexel Building. Here it remained until 1880, when it was removed to its present site into a commodious building, which has been rendered still more spacious by an extensive addition, for which it is indebted to a liberal donation from Henry C. Lea, Esq. In its management the Philadelphia Library is, and always has been, practically a *free library,* any person, though a non-member, being entitled, when within its walls, to all the privileges of the members themselves, and being allowed, under certain regulations, to take books to his home on the payment of a trifling charge. This system of free use of the books was adopted at the inception of the library, at a time when a free library had hardly been thought of anywhere. The number of volumes in the library at present is approximately one hundred and seventy-five thousand. The important branch of this institution known as "The Ridgway Branch of the Philadelphia Library," located at Broad and Christian Streets, is described on a later page.

Philadelphia Library.

PHILADELPHIA LIBRARY, LOCUST AND JUNIPER STREETS.

In this immediate vicinity, at the south-west corner of Thirteenth and Locust Streets, are the fine apartments of the **Historical Society of Pennsylvania**, formerly the mansion of the late General Robert Patterson, and after his death acquired by the Society and improved for its present purposes by the erection of an assembly-hall for meetings and the construction of fire-proof rooms for the more valuable treasures of the Society; the whole outlay aggregating about $100,000. The Society was founded in 1824; the new hall was inaugurated in 1884. The Historical Society has been diligent in the collection of the treasures of provincial lore, its library containing invaluable material for the history of Pennsylvania and elsewhere. Chief among these are the extensive Tower Collection of Colonial Laws; books printed in Philadelphia from 1685 to 1785 (seventeen hundred and ninety-six volumes); a large collection of Colonial newspapers; an extensive series of genealogies and local histories of the Middle and Southern States; American political history from 1682 to 1789 (three thousand pamphlets); ninety-four volumes of manuscripts relating to the Penn family, 1681 to 1817; and the Maclure collection of books relating to the French Revolution (eighteen hundred and ten volumes). In addition to these literary treasures, the Society possesses numerous valuable prints and paintings and a host of other relics of Colonial Pennsylvania, its rooms being amply worthy a visit from those interested in historical material.

<small>Pennsylvania Historical Society.</small>

At the north-east corner of Thirteenth and Locust Streets is the **College of Physicians of Philadelphia**, a medical association incorporated in 1789, its object being "to advance the science of medicine." Many of the foremost physicians of Philadelphia are included among its members. There is a lectureship supported by it, and at its monthly meetings addresses are delivered and papers read. From time to time volumes of Transactions are published. A very large and valuable medical library—open for use daily except Sundays and holidays—and an important museum of anatomical and pathological specimens are among the possessions of the College. The library is, with the exception of the surgeon-general's library at Washington, the largest and most complete medical library in the United States.

<small>College of Physicians.</small>

A stone's throw distant, at the north-west corner of Thirteenth and Walnut Streets, stands the plain building of the **Philadelphia Club**, probably the oldest and most exclusive social organization of

Philadelphia Club. the kind in the city, having been formed more than half a century ago, and reckoning among its members many of the leading citizens of Philadelphia. No persons residing in Philadelphia, except members, are allowed to visit the club, and no non-resident visitors are admitted except upon introduction by a member.

A few doors to the westward, on the opposite side of Walnut Street (No. 1316), is the handsome new building of the **University Club**, **University Club.** an association of some three hundred and fifty members, mostly professional gentlemen, and all college graduates. The building, designed by Mr. Wilson Eyre, is of a Spanish-Moorish style of architecture, lately coming much into vogue.

This vicinity is, indeed, to some extent, a club centre. In addition to the clubs named may be added the **Clover Club**, meeting at the Bellevue Hotel; the **Contemporary Club**, holding its sessions in the Art Club rooms; the **Acorn Club** (a ladies' association), at 1504 Walnut Street; the **Unitarian Club**, at 124 South Twelfth Street; the **Sketch Club**, at Eleventh and Walnut Streets; the **Journalists' Club**, at 904 Walnut Street; while a number of others, political or social, meet near here. At 211 South Twelfth Street is the **Philopatrian Hall**, head-quarters of the **Philopatrian Literary Institute**, an association of young men of the Roman Catholic Church which is held in high repute by that denomination.

IX.

SOUTH BROAD STREET AND VICINITY.

THAT section of Broad Street extending southward from Pine Street, and known to Philadelphians as South Broad, possesses only to a moderate degree those splendid architectural improvements that characterize the central and northern sections of that thoroughfare, though here and there through the entire extent of the built-up portions handsome churches and other public institutions and comfortable dwellings are found. In the square on Broad Street from Lombard to South Streets are some striking examples of a more or less lavish expenditure in the construction of private mansions, and in this vicinity are numerous churches of various denominations.

At the corner of Broad and Catharine Streets is that excellent institution, the **Howard Hospital and Infirmary for Incurables,** which

Howard Hospital. was founded in 1854, under the name of the "Western Clinical Infirmary," its present name having been adopted five years later. An average of about five thousand patients are registered at this hospital per annum, and more than two hundred thousand have been treated since its foundation.

Opposite the Howard Hospital, on the west side of Broad Street, extending from Christian to some distance north of Catharine, is the new site selected for the **Jefferson Medical College and Hospital,** where ample and thoroughly adapted buildings for the needs of this institution are expected to be ready for occupancy in October, 1893. Every modern convenience for a thorough medical training will be provided, so that the well-earned reputation of the College cannot but be enhanced by the change of locality.

On the east side of Broad Street, occupying the grounds bounded by Broad, Christian, Thirteenth, and Carpenter Streets, stands, in a

Ridgway Library. kind of solitary grandeur, the colossal granite edifice known as the **Ridgway Branch of the Philadelphia Library,** a bequest by the late Dr. James Rush to the Library,—a magnificent gift, embodying the proceeds of an estate of an aggregate value of about one million dollars, which have been so expended as to produce a stately monument of architecture almost, or quite, unrivalled among American library buildings. The institu-

PHILADELPHIA LIBRARY—RIDGWAY BRANCH—BROAD AND CHRISTIAN STREETS.

tion was named in the will of the donor in honor of his wife (the daughter of Jacob Ridgway, a wealthy Philadelphia merchant), from whom he received the major portion of the estate thus bequeathed. The building is finely appointed within, and is made the receptacle of the less used books and treasures of the Library, some of them of great antiquarian value; besides which, in a room set apart for the purpose, are kept certain costly articles of furniture which once belonged to Mrs. Rush, and in another apartment is contained the tomb of Dr. and Mrs. Rush.

On the east side of Broad, near Wharton Street, is the fine Armory of the Third Regiment (National Guard of Pennsylvania), whose ample

Third Regiment Armory.

interior extent admirably adapts it to drill purposes. Its great size rendered it the only building suitable for the recent grand Fair of the Teachers' Annuity Fund, whose results provided a satisfactory endowment for this praiseworthy purpose.

Several squares southward from this point, at the corner of Broad and Morris Streets, stands the new building of the **Southern Home for**

Home for Destitute Children.

Destitute Children, a highly useful charity, which has been in existence since 1841, has had over four thousand five hundred inmates, and has placed hundreds in comfortable homes. Long located at Twelfth and Fitzwater Streets, it occupied its new building in 1891. This is a spacious, four-storied structure, of light-colored brick-work, excellently adapted to its purpose, and provided with ample play-grounds for its inmates, who number about one hundred.

On the west side of Broad Street, with grounds extending from Mifflin to McKean Streets (Nos. 1900 to 2000), stands **St. Agnes's Hos-**

St. Agnes's Hospital.

pital, a Roman Catholic institution, erected through the generosity of leading members of that denomination. The building, designed in the Romanesque style of architecture, has excellent accommodations for patients, and is in every respect admirably appointed. This institution is conducted by the Tertiary Sisters of St. Francis.

Three squares south of St. Agnes's Hospital, on grounds extending from Broad Street to Thirteenth, and from Wolf Street to Ritner (Nos. 2300 to 2400 South Broad), is the site of the **Methodist Episcopal**

Methodist Hospital.

Hospital in the City of Philadelphia, which owes its existence to a bequest from Dr. Scott Stewart, a physician of Philadelphia, who died in 1881, leaving his estate "as

ST. AGNES'S HOSPITAL.

METHODIST HOSPITAL.

SOUTH BROAD STREET AND VICINITY.

a nucleus for the erection of a hospital, to be established in that part of the city south of South Street," and "to be under the auspices of the Methodist Episcopal Church." The lot contains five acres of ground, on which it is designed to erect six hospital pavilions, with a total capacity of three hundred and fifty beds. One of these, with a capacity of seventy beds, is now completed and in operation, together with an administration and other buildings. The Hospital was formally dedicated on April 21, 1892. It is open to all races and creeds, and without charge to those unable to pay, it being supported mainly by private contributions and church collections.

Broad Street extends about two miles below this point, to League Island, ending in the United States Navy-Yard at that location. Here we reach the junction of the Delaware and Schuylkill Rivers, near which, on Penrose Ferry Road, is **Point Breeze Park**, the well-known racing-grounds. There is here a well-laid, solid track, on which some of the finest trotters in this country have tried their speed. Near by, at the mouth of the Schuylkill, are the **Girard Point Elevators**, one of which has a capacity of about one million bushels of grain, the other of seven hundred and fifty thousand bushels.

Of the buildings in the vicinity of South Broad Street, the most important is the Philadelphia county prison, known as **Moyamensing Prison**, a massive square building of the Tudor style of English Gothic castle architecture. It is situated at Tenth and Reed Streets, and consists of a central square building with wings on either side, in which are accommodations for about five hundred prisoners. It is often much overcrowded, and a new county prison is now being erected on Pennypack Creek, near the House of Correction.

Moyamensing Prison.

Of the ground originally purchased for the county prison, an unused portion was long used as a parade ground, and part of this, bounded by Wharton, Reed, Twelfth, and Thirteenth Streets, has been converted into a public square, known as **Passyunk Square**,—a pleasant place of resort for the neighboring inhabitants.

MOYAMENSING PRISON.

X.

NAVAL ASYLUM AND VICINITY.

PLEASANTLY situated on the east bank of the Schuylkill River, at Bainbridge Street and Gray's Ferry Road, perhaps a mile and a half south-west of the City Hall, is the **United States Naval Asylum**, a home for those retired man-of-war's men whose term of service (twenty years) entitles them to admission. The principal buildings of the Asylum are a main edifice

Naval Asylum.

UNITED STATES NAVAL ASYLUM AND HOSPITAL.

(called the "Home"), a commodious residence for the governor of the Asylum, and a surgeon's residence,—the Home consisting of a centre building with wings at either hand, and having an entire length of three hundred and eighty feet, with accommodations for about three hundred people. On the front a flight of marble steps leads to the main entrance, where is a handsome portico of eight Ionic columns supporting a pediment. In the centre building of the Home are the chapel, opposite the entrance, and other general apartments, the rooms of the residents being in the wings, each lodger occupying a separate room, for the order of which he is responsible. A new extension on the rear is intended for rooms for the attendants. The wings are symmetrical, and terminate in pavilions, or transverse buildings, at each end furnished with broad covered verandas on each of the two main floors. A fine attic and basement complete the building, which is most substantially constructed in every part. The marble staircases are especially noticeable for their ingenious construction and economy of space. The ceilings of two floors are vaulted in solid masonry, and the room used as a muster-room and chapel is a remarkably high-domed apartment. This institution is, in the true sense of the word, an asylum,—a place of rest and recuperation for "decrepit and disabled naval officers, seamen, and marines." Within the well-kept grounds of the Asylum, about twenty-five acres in extent, is also a government **Naval Hospital**, a fine building of brick, with brown-

Naval Hospital.

stone trimmings, having accommodations for some three hundred and fifty patients, and where members of the naval service of all degrees of rank, whether belonging to this asylum or sent here from other stations, are admitted. These institutions are conveniently reached by the cars which run out Pine or South Street, and from the vicinity of Fairmount the Spruce Street cars for Gray's Ferry Bridge pass the grounds.

A short distance beyond the Naval Asylum, also on Gray's Ferry Road, surrounded by high walls of brick and stone, are the grounds

Schuylkill Arsenal.

of the **Schuylkill Arsenal**, an old-time establishment, once, perhaps, an *arsenal proper*, but now little more than a huge government clothing manufactory—giving employment to hundreds of operatives at their homes in making up army clothing. The grounds of the arsenal (about eight acres) are well laid out and shaded, the buildings are plain, the principal ones being arranged around a circular plot,—one of them, known as the museum, containing a curious collection of wax figures dressed to represent the uniforms of the United States army at various periods.

Beyond the Arsenal, on Gray's Ferry Road, near where that thoroughfare reaches the bridge across the Schuylkill River, are located extensive industrial establishments, principally devoted to the manufacture of paints, chemicals, and kindred products, the chief among which are the works of **Harrison Brothers & Co.**, whose specialties are paints, acids, etc., and the **Kalion Chemical Company**, extensive manufacturers of glycerine products.

In the vicinity of the Naval Asylum, at Twenty-second and Bainbridge Streets, is the popular **Bethany Presbyterian Church**, which is worthy of mention for its rapid increase in membership and the remarkable growth of its Sunday-school, which has nearly three thousand scholars. This noted Sunday-school building is a brown-stone Gothic structure, one hundred and thirty-eight feet by one hundred and eighty-five feet in extent, having within its walls a series of class-rooms, lecture-rooms, chapels, and other apartments. Connected with this establishment are various secular institutions, an evening school, a dispensary, etc.

<small>Bethany Church.</small>

Following the Schuylkill, at a short distance below the Naval Asylum we reach Gray's Ferry Bridge, the locality of a well-known old-time ferry, now crossed by a branch of the Pennsylvania Railroad. On the west side of the river at this point, occupying a somewhat elevated tract, is the notable **Bartram's Garden**, a locality of great interest to botanists and lovers of nature. Here, in 1731, John Bartram, the celebrated botanist, fixed his abode, the quaint old stone mansion, largely built by his own hands, being one of the interesting features of the locality. Bartram established here the most widely-known botanic garden ever opened in America. It was singularly rich in American and foreign trees and shrubs, not a few of which still remain, the most noteworthy among them being an immense cypress-tree, said to have been brought from Florida by Bartram in 1749. Bartram's Garden is now a city park, having been purchased by the city for that purpose. Its interesting features will be strictly maintained, and there is much in it worthy of a visit.

<small>Bartram's Garden.</small>

Following the Schuylkill still farther southward, we reach the locality of the extensive **Point Breeze Gas-Works**, which are situated on the east bank of the river, on the line of Passyunk Avenue. These are much the most extensive gas-works in the city, and are believed to be the largest in the world. Their equipment includes an immense telescopic gas-holder, one hundred and sixty feet in diameter and ninety-five feet high. The city possesses several other gas-works, of which the most

<small>Point-Breeze Gas-Works.</small>

important is that at Market Street wharf, on the Schuylkill River, from which the main supply of the city was received until its great growth rendered necessary a much more productive plant.

This locality is also of interest from the extensive oil refineries which are here situated, there being visible on both sides of the river groups of great iron tanks, for the storage of crude and refined oil. The pipe line from the oil region terminates at this point. The facilities for loading oil are very great. One of the largest tank steamers, with a capacity of one million five hundred thousand gallons, can be loaded in ten hours. These oil-works have been the scene of several extensive fires, among the most destructive that have visited the city of recent years. But the business is too important to let the ravages of fire diminish its activity, and each conflagration is quickly followed by a rebuilding, with improved and increased productive facilities.

Oil Refineries.

XI.

BROAD AND SPRING GARDEN STREETS AND VICINITY.

THE vicinity of Broad and Spring Garden Streets, for decades devoted to a class of industries which have made the locality famous, is still the home of many of those gigantic concerns which years ago gave it its reputation. Here, prominent among their surroundings, and eminently worthy of their world-wide fame, are the **Baldwin Locomotive-Works**, now under the proprietorship of Burnham, Williams & Co., a vast establishment, which was founded in 1831 by Matthias W. Baldwin, and has grown from an humble origin into the immense industry which so honorably perpetuates the name of its founder. The works at present cover an area of fourteen acres, and employ nearly five thousand men, while they have the enormous productive capacity of one thousand locomotives a year. In 1892 the firm completed its *thirteen thousandth* locomotive. The principal departments of these works run continuously, night and day, they being lighted by two thousand eight hundred electric lamps. It is an interesting fact that the lightest locomotive built in these works weighed five thousand one hundred pounds, the heaviest one hundred and ninety-five thousand pounds; or seventy-six tons (about one hundred tons with the tender). This establishment is the largest locomotive-building works in the world, and one of the leading points of attraction to strangers visiting the city.

Several other extensive, and numerous small, industrial establishments add to the interest of this vicinity. On Hamilton Street, extending from Sixteenth to Seventeenth Streets, is the extensive machine-tool manufactory of **William Sellers & Co.**, founded in 1848, and one of the largest of its kind in the country. On Callowhill Street, with the same extent, are the **Whitney Car-Wheel Works**, which are equally notable in their specialty. At Sixteenth and Buttonwood Streets are the **Bush Hill Iron-Works**, engaged in the production of boilers and heavy furnace equipments. Various other industrial establishments may be seen in this neighborhood, while east of Broad Street occur numerous others, the most important of

them being the extensive **Hoopes & Townsend Bolt-Works**, on Buttonwood Street east from Broad, in which this branch of manufacture is conducted on the largest scale.

In addition to its importance as an industrial centre, the vicinity of Broad and Spring Garden Streets is also notable as an educational centre, the high and normal schools of the public-school system, with other prominent educational institutions, being located here.

At No. 1336 Spring Garden Street are the class-rooms of "**The Pennsylvania Museum and School of Industrial Art**," an institution

School of Industrial Art.
incorporated in 1876, "with a special view to the development of the art industries of the State." Here is given instruction in drawing from casts and models; in wood-carving; in weaving and textile design, including the construction of looms; in chemistry and dyeing; in decorative painting, including the grinding and preparation of colors; in modelling, etc. Connected with this institution is the museum at Memorial Hall, in Fairmount Park. The present building being too contracted for the purposes of the School, it is designed to remove it, in the near future, to a more suitable locality. At the north-east corner of Broad and Spring Garden Streets stands the building of the **Spring Garden Institute**, a semi-charitable institution, which maintains

Spring Garden Institute.
a library and free reading-room, courses of free lectures and entertainments, night-schools in drawing and mechanical handiwork at a nominal fee, and day-schools in drawing and painting at a charge to pupils of about the cost of maintenance. To these has been recently added a day-school for the purpose of instruction in general wood- and metal-work. The number of pupils in the session of 1891-92 was seven hundred and eighty-seven, mainly engaged in the study of drawing.

One square north, at the south-east corner of Broad and Green Streets, is the **Central High School**, for boys, a plain brick structure,

Central High School.
erected in 1854, with accommodations for about six hundred and fifty students. In addition to the usual class-rooms, the building possesses an observatory, with astronomical instruments. This building has become inadequate for its purpose, and an extension, or replacement by a new school building, is contemplated. The course of study occupies four years.

Not far removed from the High School are two more recent

structures for a similar purpose, the **Girls' Normal Schools.** The earlier of these, that situated at Seventeenth and Spring Garden Streets, is a spacious structure of green serpentine, five stories high, and with class-room for more than fifteen hundred pupils. Adjoining and connected with this is a **School of Practice** (in the art of teaching), capable of containing about six hundred pupils, making in all over two thousand scholars under one administration. To this is now being added another school of equal dimensions, at the north-west corner of Thirteenth and Spring Garden Streets, replacing the well-known Spring Garden Hall. This is a massive and spacious granite building, four stories high, and covering a ground space of one hundred and fifty by one hundred and seventy-eight feet. Interiorly forty class-rooms and accommodations for two thousand pupils have been provided, together with the best modern conveniences for school purposes. It will be ready for use in the 1893-94 school year, when the School of Practice will be transferred to this building.

Girls' Normal Schools.

Another important adjunct of the high-school system of Philadelphia is the newly-established **Manual Training-School,** at Seventeenth and Wood Streets. The purpose of this department of the public-school system (opened in 1885) is "to afford to pupils who have finished the grammar-school course the opportunity not only to pursue the usual High-School course in literature, science, and mathematics, but also to receive a thorough course in drawing, and in the use and application of tools in the industrial arts." The prescribed order of exercises is to give "one hour per day to drawing, two hours to shop-work, and three hours to the usual academic studies." This school has proved so popular that it has been found necessary to open another of the same class, on Howard Street, below Girard Avenue, and still others may before long become necessary.

Manual Training-School.

Of buildings devoted to other purposes than industry and education in this vicinity, one of the most striking is the new club-house of the **Caledonian Club,** at the north-east corner of Spring Garden and Thirteenth Streets, a handsome and roomy structure, six stories high and with ample ground area. It is built of brick and red sandstone, and contains, in addition to the club-rooms, a gymnasium, running track, swimming-pool, bowling-alley, and all the requisites of a first-class club-house. The club is an athletic society, devoted to Scottish games.

Caledonian Club.

On the north side of Spring Garden Street, west of Thirteenth, is the **Lu Lu Temple**, occupying the former St. Philip's Church, which has been adapted to the purposes of the Order. This Order is affiliated with that of the Free Masons to the extent that every member must be a Mason, though beyond this there is no connection.

On Broad Street, at the corner of Callowhill, is the **Armory of the First Regiment National Guards of Pennsylvania**, a castellated Gothic building three stories in height. The base of the structure is of rock-faced mason-work surmounted by walls of brick, the trimmings to the windows and doors, etc., being of dressed stone. The principal entrance on Broad Street is flanked by two towers rising to a height of one hundred and twenty feet. The front or main building is sixty-five by one hundred and thirty-eight feet, and contains officers' rooms, and companies' rooms, squad drill-room, drum-corps room, kitchen, and billiard-room, besides dressing-rooms and store-rooms. The drill-room on the first floor is one hundred and thirty-nine by one hundred and fifty-five feet, with gun-racks at the eastern end, and a gallery for visitors at the western end.

Northward on Broad Street are a number of churches, of which the most striking in architectural effect is the Hebrew Synagogue, **Rodef Shalom**, at the corner of Mount Vernon Street. This is built of stone of various colors, and presents a fine example of Saracenic architecture. Farther north, at the corner of Fairmount Avenue, is the **Park Theatre**, a well-appointed place of amusement, with seats for twenty-two hundred persons. Diagonally opposite, on the south-west corner of Broad Street and Fairmount Avenue, is the attractive building of the **American Trust Company and Saving Fund**, which presents an odd and effective combination of granite and brown-stone.

XII.

NORTH BROAD STREET AND VICINITY.

NORTH BROAD STREET, the finest section of one of the finest thoroughfares in the world, is pre-eminently a street of luxurious homes and handsome churches. Among its dwellings there are not a few which, for architectural excellence, are well worthy of remark. It is rendered more attractive by its many beautiful gardens, open in whole or in part to the street, and by its wide and smooth asphalt pavement, which makes this avenue one of the favorite carriage-drives of Philadelphia. As a whole, this section of Broad Street is one that has few rivals in American cities.

In passing up this avenue, above the section already reviewed, numbers of fine churches are met, while of other institutions the first encountered is the **Children's Homœopathic Hospital**, situated on Broad Street below Girard Avenue. It has a dispensary for both children and adults. At 1240 North Broad Street is **La Salle College** (Roman Catholic). It was incorporated in 1863, occupies excellent and ample buildings, and takes rank as one of the best institutions of its class in the city.

At the south-west corner of Broad and Master Streets stands the large and well-adapted building of the **Philadelphia School of Design for Women**, the foremost institution of its kind in this country. Founded in 1847, it was established in 1863 at the corner of Merrick and Filbert Streets. This property being taken for the new Pennsylvania Railroad Station, the Edwin Forrest mansion, at Broad and Master Streets, was purchased and adapted to the purposes of the School by the building of a large additional structure. The institution, which has several hundred pupils, is in a flourishing condition, giving full instruction in the various branches of industrial art and in the elements of the fine arts. It is well worth a visit by all interested in the higher education of women.

A short distance above, at the north-west corner of Broad and Oxford Streets, is the new edifice of the **Columbia Club**, one of the handsomest club buildings in the city. It is built of light-buff brick, with brown-stone base and trimmings. At Broad Street and Columbia Avenue stands the ornate and attractive building of the **Columbia Avenue Savings-Fund, Safe Deposit, Title and Trust Company.** Just above, at the corner of Broad Street and Montgomery Avenue, may be seen the **Grand Opera House,** one of the largest and most comfortable places of amusement in the city, and a favorite place of resort for the admirers of summer opera. Directly opposite this building are two churches which are worthy of special mention. On the south-east corner of Montgomery Avenue is the **Church of the Messiah** (Universalist), a beautifully ornate Gothic stone structure. Adjoining it on the south is the new **Keneseth Israel Synagogue,** of the Reformed Israelite congregation, hitherto located at Sixth and Brown Streets. This edifice is built of Indiana limestone, in the Italian Renaissance style, has a front of one hundred and twenty feet on Broad Street, with a handsome campanile one hundred and twenty feet in height, and a cut-glass central dome of one hundred and twelve feet in height. The edifice presents a highly-attractive appearance. It has seats for about seventeen hundred persons.

At the south-east corner of Broad and Berks Street stands the widely-known **Grace Baptist Church,** one of the largest, most elaborate, and most costly places of worship in the United States. This edifice, locally known as "The Temple," is a Romanesque building, of Avondale limestone, with Indiana limestone trimmings, and is a great ornament to the section of the city where it stands. It has seats for over three thousand people. Connected with this church is **Temple College,** in which instruction is given to a large number of young persons at a very moderate cost. Directly opposite Grace Church is the main entrance to the **Monument Cemetery,** so named from the fine monument in its centre to the memory of Washington and Lafayette. On the west side of Broad Street, above Diamond Street, is the location designed for the new armory of the **Second Regiment National Guards of Pennsylvania,** at present located in the National Guards' Hall, Race Street near Sixth. There has been secured here a lot three hundred and five feet front by two hundred feet deep, on which it is proposed to erect a building equal in its facilities for drill and other regimental requirements to the best armories now in existence, and

MASONIC HOME OF PENNSYLVANIA.

defensible against any ordinary attack. It will probably be built during the year 1893.

Farther north may be seen several institutions of interest in the vicinity of Broad Street. These are chiefly of a charitable character, though among them is the **Philadelphia Base-Ball Park**, the spacious and well-appointed grounds of the Philadelphia Club, and the favorite place of resort in Philadelphia for the many lovers of this specially American game. It is situated at Fifteenth and Huntingdon Streets.

Base-Ball Park.

On Lehigh Avenue, at the corner of Twenty-first Street, stands the **Municipal Hospital**, a city institution for the treatment of small-pox and other infectious diseases. It succeeds the City Hospital founded in 1818, and situated on Fairmount Avenue from Nineteenth to Twentieth Streets. The present building was occupied in 1865. It is a large stone edifice, with a front length of two hundred and eighty feet.

Municipal Hospital.

Not far distant, at Twentieth Street and Lehigh Avenue, are the Medical, Surgical, and Maternity Hospitals of the **Women's Homœopathic Association of Philadelphia**, an institution under the control of a board of women managers, and receives paying and non-paying patients of any creed and color.

On the east side of Broad Street, above Ontario Street, may be seen the edifice of a recently-established institution, the **Samaritan Hospital**, founded in 1891 by Rev. Russell H. Conwell, of the Grace Baptist Church. The Hospital occupies a large double house of fourteen rooms, surrounded by grounds which are tastefully laid out in flower-beds, lawns, walks, etc., the whole establishment seeming rather like a private home than an hospital. It was opened for patients on February 1, 1892, with a capacity of twenty beds and a dispensary department. The need of such an institution is shown by the fact that it is occupied to its full capacity. Persons of any creed, nationality, or color are admitted.

On Lehigh Avenue, between Thirteenth and Broad Streets, is the **Home for Aged and Infirm Methodists**, an excellent example of institutions of its class. It has accommodation for about one hundred inmates, and occupies spacious and handsome stone buildings.

On Broad Street north of Clearfield (Nos. 3331 to 3337) is the **Masonic Home of Pennsylvania**, an institution founded in 1884 as the "Home for Free and Accepted Masons." The number of inmates at date of last report was twenty-

Masonic Home.

ODD-FELLOWS' HOME.

HOME FOR ORPHANS OF ODD-FELLOWS OF PENNSYLVANIA.

nine, constituting the few persons subject to charitable care of the forty-two thousand Masons of Pennsylvania. The institution is supported by voluntary contributions from members and Lodges.

Another institution worthy of note in the vicinity of North Broad Street is the **Odd-Fellows' Home**, at Seventeenth and Tioga Streets, established in 1875, and one of the best institutions of its class. No money has been spent here for architectural effect, but all contributions have been devoted to the purpose intended. This Home is not in any proper sense a charity, as each inmate has paid for years into an annuity fund, and has a claim to admission. It contains at present about sixty inmates. There is attached to it an infirmary building. Not far distant, at Twentieth and Ontario Streets, is the **Home for Orphans of Odd-Fellows**, an institution incorporated in 1883. It is supported by voluntary contributions, and contains about fifty children. The lot is two hundred and fifty feet square, affording ample room for playgrounds. The institution is free from debt, and there will be added in the near future a play-house and an infirmary.

<small>Odd-Fellows' Home.</small>

Farther south, in the section west of Broad Street, are two institutions worthy of notice. At Seventeenth and Norris Streets, occupying a large and picturesque stone building, is the **Baptist Home for Women**. This building was occupied nineteen years ago, and is neatly and comfortably appointed, with pleasant grounds and home-like rooms. It has a capacity for eighty-one inmates.

<small>Baptist Home for Women.</small>

On Seventeenth Street, at the corner of Montgomery Avenue, stands an important scientific institution, the **Wagner Free Institute of Science**, a large building containing a valuable library, an extensive biological museum, and scientific laboratories. Connected with it is a lecture-hall, in which courses of free scientific lectures are given. A branch of the City Free Library and a centre of the University Extension Association are located here. There has also been recently opened here a free public library, one of several designed to be opened by the city as accessories to the public-school system. This institution was founded in 1855 by William Wagner, its purpose being free popular instruction in science.

<small>Wagner Institute.</small>

Worthy of mention, also, is the **Howard Institution**, situated at No. 1612 Poplar Street, its purpose being "the assistance, reformation, and shelter of destitute women released from prison or otherwise homeless." This charity has proved a very useful one.

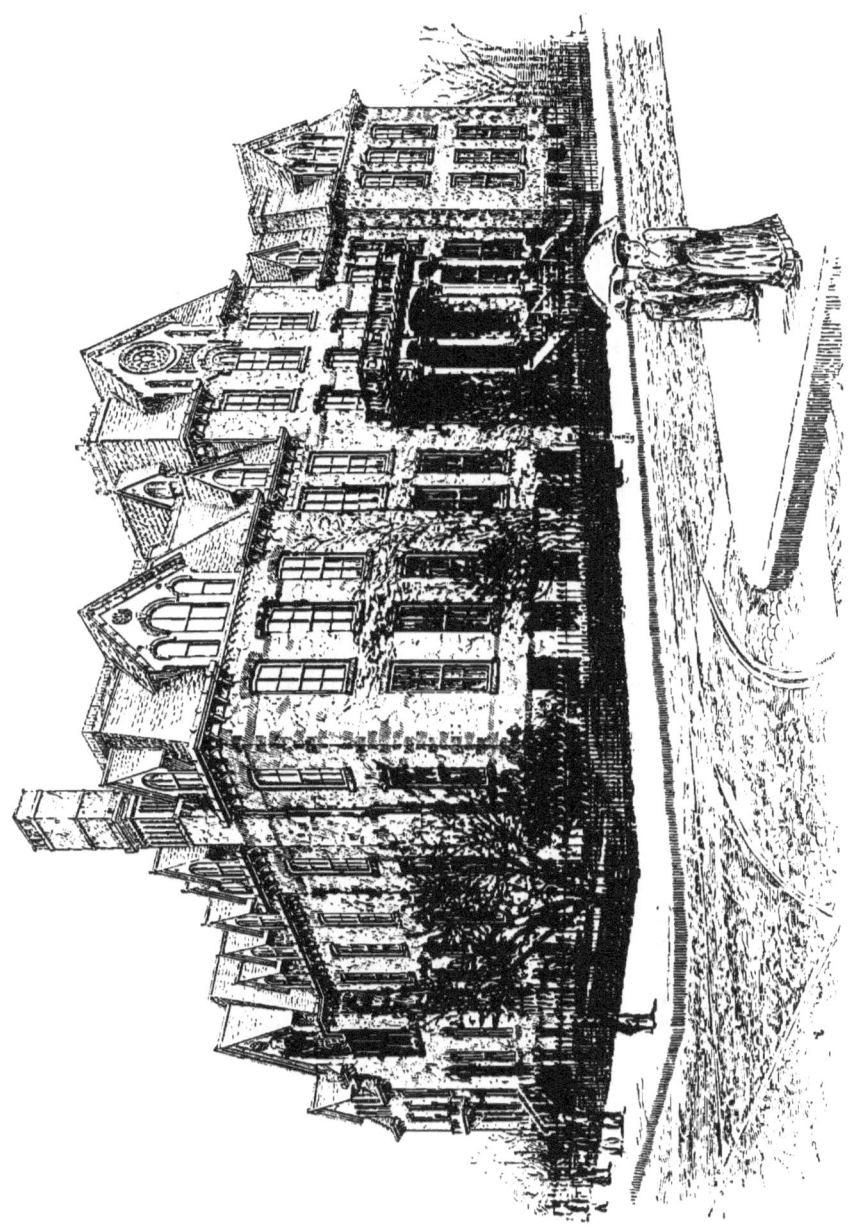

XIII.

GIRARD COLLEGE AND VICINITY.

GIRARD COLLEGE stands in the centre of a very interesting and important group of public and private charitable institutions, the most important of which are here noticed.

The **Girard College Buildings** occupy a space of forty-one acres, extending from Nineteenth Street and Girard Avenue, along Ridge Avenue and westward to Twenty-fifth Street, the grounds being surrounded by a high wall. The main building is among the finest extant examples of Corinthian architecture; and the other buildings are on a grand scale. Probably no institution in Philadelphia is more talked of and excites a more general interest; certainly none is more visited by strangers. The College was founded by Stephen Girard, who, dying in 1830, gave the specific sum of two million dollars to build the College, and left the greater part of his estate to endow it. The original buildings were fourteen years in construction, the corner-stone having been laid in 1833 and the main building finished in 1847. It was designed by the late Thomas U. Walter, and its transcendant beauty and great magnificence are everywhere acknowledged, it having, as a piece of monumental architecture, scarcely a rival on this continent. The principal buildings in the enclosure are of white marble, and the more lately built among them are most admirably adapted to their main educational purposes.

<small>Girard College.</small>

The College was established for the education of poor white male orphans, from six to ten years old at the time of their admittance, preference being given, first, to those born within the limits of the *old* city of Philadelphia; second, to natives of Pennsylvania; third, to boys born in New York; and, fourth, to those born in New Orleans. At present about fifteen hundred and fifty orphans are being cared for and trained in Girard College. There are in all ten auxiliary buildings, a handsome chapel, etc. The grounds are ample for the recreation and athletic and military training of the boys, and are well worthy of a visit each summer for the highly beautiful floral and foliage decoration of the lawn fronting the main building.

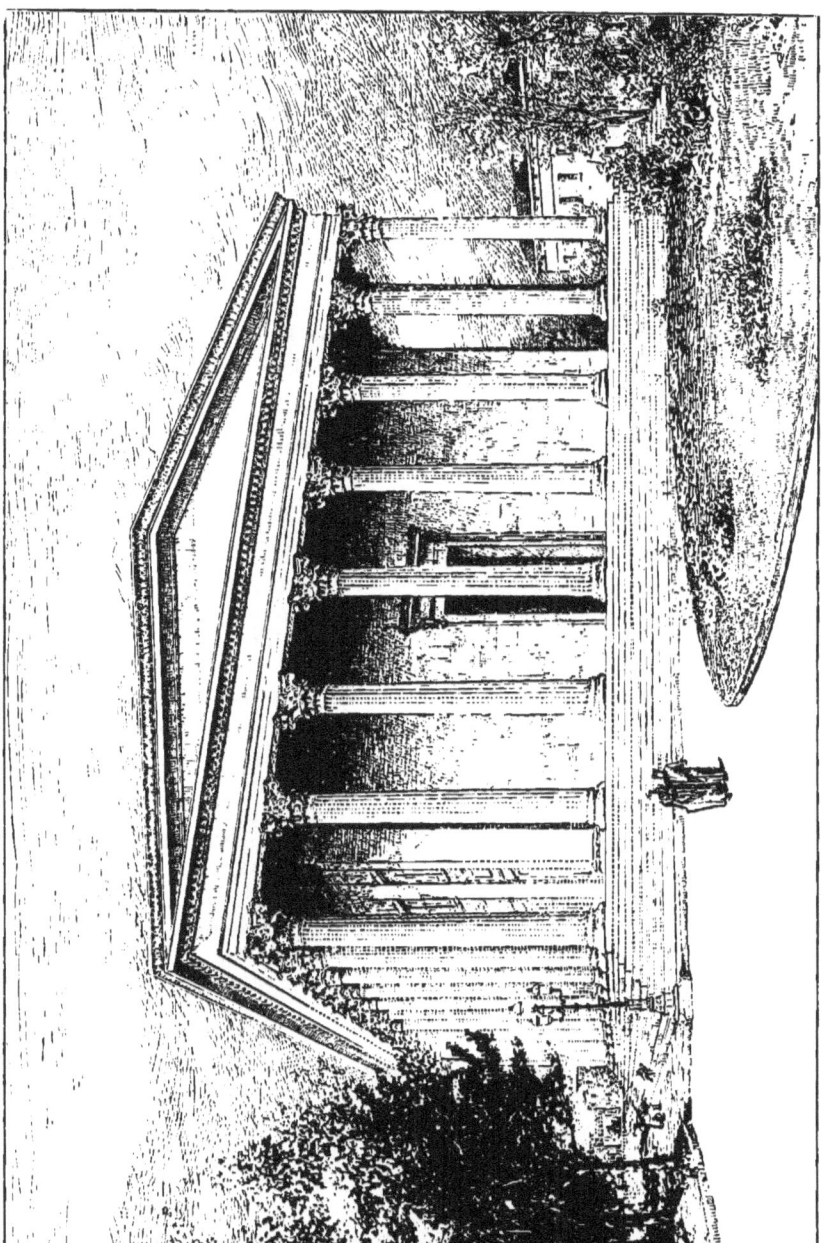

The **German Hospital**, at the south-west corner of Girard and Corinthian Avenues, is a handsome structure of stone. It was founded in 1860, largely by the liberality of citizens of German birth, and, during the war of 1861-65, was used as a United States military hospital. It was reopened as a general hospital for public uses in 1866. Both German and English are spoken, and patients of any nationality whatsoever may be admitted. The nurses are German Deaconesses from the **Mary J. Drexel Home** and Philadelphia Mother-House of Deaconesses, which stands in the same enclosure with the hospital, and on the south side of Girard Avenue, just west of the Hospital itself. The Drexel Home was founded in 1888 by Mr. John D. Lankenau, in memory of his deceased wife, *née* Mary J. Drexel, a daughter of the founder of the house of Drexel & Co., and sister of the eminent bankers of that name. It is a noble and beautiful building of yellow brick, imported from Germany, and trimmed with facings of gray sandstone. It is of a Gothic architecture, modified by details in the Norman style; the main stairways and some of the floors are of white marble. Connected with this great institution is a school for Deaconesses. The building includes a children's hospital, children's home, and a home for aged people.

German Hospital.

Drexel Home.

At the north-west corner of Twenty-first Street and North College Avenue stand the handsome and commodious buildings of the **Women's Medical College**, the first medical school especially for women ever established in the world. Its faculty includes both men and women physicians, and it has graduated a large number of highly-successful lady practitioners. Very near to it stands the **Women's Hospital**, where women and children alone are treated. Its buildings at present are ample for its purposes. Both medical and surgical cases are here treated, and the hospital has proved itself an extremely praiseworthy institution. Both the College and Hospital, which are closely affiliated to each other, are to-day in a high tide of successful work.

Women's Medical College.

At a short distance north-east from the eastern extremity of the Girard College grounds, extending on Stiles Street from Seventeenth to Eighteenth Streets, stands one of the largest ecclesiastical establishments in Philadelphia,—the **Church of the Gesù**, under the care of a body of Jesuit priests. The church itself is a great and lofty pile of brick and marble, with granite foundations. The interior is beautifully decorated, and the

The Church of the Gesù.

THE MARY J. DREXEL HOME, GIRARD AVENUE, NEAR TWENTY-SECOND STREET.

roof of the nave is a wonderfully fine piece of barrel-vaulting. This great church is well worthy of a visit. Connected with it are large parochial schools. A part of the same establishment is **St. Joseph's College**, of which the members of the faculty all belong to the order of the Jesuits. Near at hand, and under the pastoral care of the clergy of the Church of the Gesù, is **St. Joseph's Hospital** (Girard Avenue, below Seventeenth Street). This is a large and very important hospital. More than a third of the cases treated are charity patients. On Girard Avenue, directly opposite the Hospital, is the **Green Hill Presbyterian Church**, of brown-stone, a handsome and capacious structure. A short walk to the northward brings us to the **Home for the Aged of Both Sexes**, on Eighteenth Street near Jefferson, a large Roman Catholic charity, under the direct care of a community of celibate women known as "The Little Sisters of the Poor," and under the pastoral charge of the Jesuit Fathers from the Church of the Gesù. This most deserving and useful institution receives the aged poor of whatever creed or nationality, without fee or reward. It occupies a large and lofty edifice of brick. This institution has a large and very important establishment in Germantown.

St. Joseph's Hospital.

Little Sisters of the Poor.

The location between Parish and Poplar, Twenty-second and Twenty-third Streets, was until recently occupied by the **House of Refuge**, for the reclamation of idle and depraved children. The principal portion of this institution, that devoted to boys, was in 1892 removed to Glen Mills, Delaware County (which see). That portion devoted to girls (white and colored) is retained in this locality, occupying a large stone building on Twenty-second Street, between Poplar Street and Girard Avenue. This institution was founded in 1826. The inmates receive careful mental and physical training.

In the vicinity of the College are several other important charitable and public institutions. On Brown Street, between Twenty-second and Twenty-third Streets, is the **Northern Home for Friendless Children**, an institution incorporated in 1854 for the care of vagrant, neglected, or abandoned children. It occupies a large building, with ample grounds, and had, at date of last report, one hundred and thirty-seven inmates. Just north of this institution, and now associated with it, is the **Soldiers' and Sailors' Orphans' Home**, its inmates now reduced to fifty-six. These Homes have done and are doing excellent work, their inmates

Northern Home for Children.

being educated, taught useful industries, and in many cases provided with permanent homes.

At Twenty-fourth and Poplar Streets, very near to Girard College, stands the **Foster Home**, the object of which "is to extend aid to respectable widowed parents who, from adversity, are obliged to part with their children for a time, but desire to have them finally restored." One hundred children can be cared for here. The parents or friends of the children are expected to defray a part of the expense of their support.

Foster Home.

Directly east of the House of Refuge is the **Corinthian Avenue Reservoir**. One square to the south we see the ponderous and frowning walls of the large **Eastern Penitentiary**, a State prison, and one of the most celebrated of its class. It occupies eleven acres of ground, lying between Brown Street and Fairmount Avenue, and extending westward from Corinthian Avenue to Twenty-second Street. Its castellated entrance, flanked and surmounted with grandly majestic towers, is very impressive. It was built in 1823–29, and was for many years conducted on the so-called "Pennsylvania System" of strictly solitary confinement; but this system has been gradually mitigated, as a necessary result of a surplus of inmates, and at present some minor degree of association of prisoners is permitted. Means are also employed to instruct the prisoners, especially the younger ones, in various useful employments. The excellent non-sectarian **Home for Aged Couples**, at the corner of Perkiomen and Francis Streets, is a chartered institution, dating from 1876.

Eastern Penitentiary.

In this vicinity may be seen one of those great industrial works for which Philadelphia is so famous. This is the **Keystone Watch-Case Works**, occupying large buildings at Nineteenth and Wylie Streets. It is one of the largest and most complete manufactories devoted to its special purpose in the world, and its annual product is a very large one.

Keystone Watch-Case Works.

XIV.

CENTRAL DELAWARE-RIVER FRONT AND VICINITY.

THAT portion of the city fronting upon the Delaware River which, from its location as well as from its comparative importance, may be termed the *Central River Front*, occupies essentially the section of the river margin included in the plot which, two hundred years ago, William Penn laid out as the site of his "great towne," and which extended from Vine Street on the north to South Street on the south, a distance of about one mile. Within these limits, in the vicinity of the wharves, are now to be found heavy business-houses which occupy all the streets great and small, and here, through the medium of their lines of ferry-boats, plying to Camden on the opposite side of the river, are the terminal stations of the several railways that connect Philadelphia with the seashore and intermediate points. Chief among these is the station of the **West Jersey Railroad**, at the foot of

West Jersey Railroad. | Market Street (now controlled by the Pennsylvania Railroad), by the side of which is the Camden Ferry, for the accommodation of teams and passengers other than those destined for the cars. Several lines of river-steamers and coasting-vessels also have their landings here, the more important of the latter being the **Clyde Lines** (the offices of which are at No. 12 South Delaware Avenue) and the principal of the former being the **Ericsson Line**, whose vessels leave daily (piers No. 7 North Delaware Avenue and No. 28 South Delaware Avenue) for Baltimore, the **Bristol Line** (Columbia and Twilight), daily from Chestnut Street wharf, the **Trenton Line** (Edwin Forrest), daily from Arch Street wharf, the **Salem (New Jersey) Line** (Reybold), daily, except Sundays, from Arch Street wharf, the **Chester and Wilmington Line**, daily from Chestnut Street wharf, the **Chester Freight Line**, from Race Street wharf, and the **Bush** and the **Warner Wilmington Steam-Packet Lines**, both of which began operation, as sailing-packet lines, considerably more than a century ago.

The **Camden and Atlantic Railroad**, the pioneer line that, by its construction to Atlantic City nearly twoscore years ago, first made conveniently accessible to Philadelphia the neighboring sea-coast of

PHILADELPHIA AND READING RAILROAD STATION, PIER 8, SOUTH DELAWARE AVENUE.

New Jersey, is now controlled by the Pennsylvania Railroad Company, and has its station at Market Street wharf, as have also lines to Mount Holly, Trenton, and other points.

A short distance below the Market Street Ferries, at Pier No. 8 South Wharves, midway between Chestnut and Walnut Streets, is the principal Philadelphia station of the Atlantic City

Reading's Atlantic City Division.

division of the Reading Railroad, whence ferry-boats connect with trains at Kaighn's Point below, on the opposite side of the Delaware. This station is conveniently reached by the Market, the Chestnut and Walnut, and the Spruce and Pine Streets lines of street cars. The Reading Railroad Company is also represented farther north, at the foot of Willow Street, where it has an extensive freight station, which connects with the main line of the road by tracks up Willow Street, and with eastern freight lines by tracks to Third and Berks Streets. Of the various industrial establishments in this vicinity, the most notable for extent is the great brewery of **John F. Betz & Son**, the second in size in the city, within whose walls malt liquors are produced in enormous quantities.

An institution of somewhat gruesome interest is **The Morgue**,

The Morgue.

which is situated on Noble Street, between Front Street and Delaware Avenue. A change of location has been decided upon. Here are taken the bodies of all unknown persons found dead, where they are kept for several days open to inspection, for recognition by relatives or friends if possible.

Prominent among the objects of interest in the vicinity of Front and Market Streets is the old **Christ Church**, on Second Street above Market, a unique brick structure on the site of a church erected in

Christ P.E.Church.

1695, and itself built in 1727–31 and enlarged at various times during the last century. This church is sixty feet in width by ninety feet in length, and has a brick tower surmounted by a wooden steeple one hundred and ninety feet high. Here in colonial days the royal officers attended public worship, and after the Revolutionary War, while Philadelphia was the seat of government, the President of the United States and other officials occupied pews in this church. The steeple contains a chime of bells cast in London about the middle of the last century. In the grounds adjoining the church are the graves of several distinguished men, and in the church-yard proper, at Fifth and Arch Streets, many eminent men have been interred.

CHRIST CHURCH.

The **Corn Exchange National Bank**, at the corner of Chestnut and Second Streets, chartered in 1858, occupies a spacious brick building, near which are the **Produce National Bank** (No. 104 Chestnut Street) and the **National Bank of Commerce**, whose home is in a plain brownstone structure (No. 209 Chestnut Street) of tasteful appearance. A square away, at the corner of Second and Walnut Streets, is the Philadelphia office of the **Camden National Bank**. Among the most imposing edifices in this vicinity is the **Commercial Exchange**, at No. 133 South Second Street, built on the site of the "Slate-Roof House," once the home of William Penn. Here in the spacious main hall, which occupies the entire upper floor of the building, meet daily (except on Sundays and legal holidays) the leading merchants and manufacturers of the city, who conduct large business operations by means of samples of their products. In the building is a station of the Postal-Telegraph Cable Company, and frequent reports of the state of the market, at home and abroad, are furnished to the Exchange. On the opposite side of Second Street is the massive government warehouse, known as the **United States Appraiser's Building**, extending from Second to Dock Streets, five stories in height, where imported goods are received from the custom-house for appraisement.

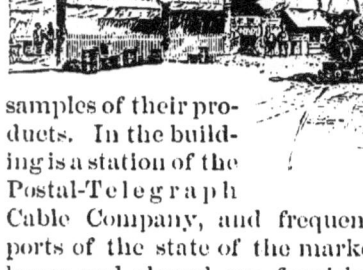

FISH AND PRODUCE BUSINESS, DELAWARE AVENUE.

The section of the city lying along the Delaware River southward from Walnut Street is largely devoted to heavy traffic by river and by rail, vast amounts of the products of the sea (fish, oysters, etc.) and of fruits and vegetables, from neighboring States and foreign lands, here finding their entrance into the city, and corresponding amounts of merchandise finding their exit from the city through the various transportation lines that have their termini here. Indeed, the fish and oyster trade principally, the produce business largely, and the fruit business almost exclusively, find along the wharves their natural entrepôt. Vast quantities of butter, cheese, vegetables, and cured meats are sold both at wholesale and retail; and

FISH AND OYSTER BUSINESS (AN INTERIOR).

in their season the peaches of Maryland and Delaware and the small fruits of New Jersey are here displayed in great abundance. Foreign fruits are brought by fast steamers in great quantities, rapidity of transportation enabling them to be marketed in excellent condition. Both fresh vegetables and fruits, however, have to be promptly handled on arrival, so that by night, as well as by day, the wharves devoted to this trade present a lively scene.

A great freight depot of the Pennsylvania Railroad extends from

FRUIT BUSINESS AT NIGHT.

Walnut Street south on Delaware Avenue to near Dock Street, and directly opposite the depot are the piers to and from which are floated, on barges, the incoming and outgoing freight trains of the West Jersey and New York divisions of the Pennsylvania Railroad. At Delaware Avenue and Spruce Street is the extensive establishment of the **Quaker City Cold Storage Company**, in effect a mammoth refrigerator constructed with all the most approved appliances for the preservation of perishable foods, having a front of one hundred feet on Delaware Avenue by a depth of one hundred and twenty-five feet on Spruce Street. It is seven stories in height, and is arranged for the entrance on the first floor of loaded refrigerator cars, from which the freights are removed to the several apartments of the building. These

SHAD-FISHING, GLOUCESTER.

establishments are reached by trains up Delaware Avenue from Washington Avenue, the latter crossing the southern section of the city from the Schuylkill to the Delaware. At the foot of Pine Street is the pier of the well-known Winsor line of steamers for Boston (reached by the Lombard Street cars), to which port semi-weekly trips are made, and near here, at the foot of South Street, is one of the terminal stations of the Atlantic City division of the Philadelphia and Reading Railroad, whence passengers are conveyed on railroad ferry-boats to Kaighn's Point to board the trains for Atlantic City and intermediate places. Adjoining this station is the Gloucester Ferry-House, the terminus of a ferry-line to Gloucester, New Jersey, a manufacturing city some three miles distant, principally celebrated for its shad-fisheries and its planked-shad dinners, which, in their season, especially endear the place to epicurean Philadelphians. This immediate locality is reached from the north and south by the cars of the Second and Third Streets line; from the west by the Spruce Street cars, which run to Third and Spruce Streets, and the Lombard Street cars, which run to Front Street; and from the north-west by the Race Street cars, which run to Second and Walnut Streets. Near here, at Third and Pine Streets, is the famous old **St. Peter's Protestant Episcopal Church**, erected before the Revolutionary War (1758–61) by the vestry and members of Christ Church, by whom it continued to be governed until 1832. Its grounds extend from Third Street to Fourth Street, and contain the graves of many distinguished citizens of the olden time. Opposite the grounds of St. Peter's (in its church-yard at the south-west corner of Fourth and Pine Streets) stands the **Third Presbyterian Church**, familiarly known as the "Old Pine Street Church," a rough-cast brick structure with a Corinthian portico of eight pillars, first opened for worship in 1768, and subsequently the scene of the pastoral labors of several eminent clergymen.

XV.

South Delaware-River Front and Vicinity.

The vicinity of the Delaware River extending from South Street to the extreme southern limit of the built-up portions of the city contains but a comparatively few objects of interest to the sight-seer, even if that vicinity be held to include all the portion of the city east of the section of this work entitled "South Broad Street and Vicinity," to which the line of Eleventh Street may be considered as a general eastern limit.

Scattered here and there, especially near the bank of the Delaware, may be found some heavy industrial works, such as are usually placed near navigable waters, prominent among which are the extensive sugar refineries of **Harrison, Frazier & Co.** and **E. C. Knight & Co.**, whose lofty buildings, near Front and Bainbridge Streets, are so nearly contiguous as to form an almost unbroken group, and whose products aggregate some five thousand barrels of refined sugar per day. These extensive establishments, which have now been absorbed by the Sugar Trust, are greatly surpassed in amount of product by the enormous refineries recently established by **Claus Spreckles**, which occupy the space between Reed, Dickinson, and Swanson Streets, and the Delaware River, covering an area of about ten acres. The buildings are of brick, are about one hundred and thirty feet high, and six acres in area. They embrace two filter-houses, finishing-house, pan-house, boiler-house, barrel-factory, machine-shops, and warehouse, while attached to the works are three six-hundred-feet wharves. These works have an enormous productive capacity. They also have been absorbed by the Sugar Trust. Southward from this point are several industrial establishments, among which **Baugh & Sons' Chemical Works** and **Taylor's Tin-Plate Works** are worthy of mention.

Sugar Refineries.

At the foot of Washington Avenue is a large grain-elevator, with a storage capacity of half a million bushels. It belongs to the Girard Point Storage Company, whose great elevators on the Schuylkill have already been mentioned. The grain cars of the Pennsylvania Railroad, crossing the city by way of Washington Avenue, discharge their freight into this elevator, whence the grain is loaded into vessels, lying at the wharf on the Delaware River. Here also is the pier (No. 47 South Delaware Avenue) of the **American Steamship Line** (now consolidated with the Inman and Red Star Lines under the name of the International Navigation Company), whose vessels sail for Liverpool on Wednesday of each week.

The line of the Delaware farther south presents no object of interest. It borders the low-lying locality known as "The Neck," a region of truck-farms and other suburban industries, and its chief importance is the opportunity it offers for future wharfage. Railroad freight tracks extend to isolated points on the river-bank, from which heavy shipments of coal and kindred products are made. A section of this locality is the property of the Cramps' ship-building company, and may in the near future become the seat of a busy shipyard, in the rapid increase of the work of this great concern. The South Delaware section reaches its terminus at League Island, the seat of the United States Navy-Yard, which is elsewhere described.

Notable among the church edifices in the south-eastern section of the city is the **Old Swedes' Church** (*Gloria Dei*), which stands on Swanson Street, below Christian, in the old district of Southwark, the Wicacoa of the Swedes. This venerable edifice was built in 1700, to take the place of a log structure which was erected in 1677, and which served equally well for church or fort, as the exigencies of those somewhat uncertain times might demand. The church is of brick, and is still regularly used. It stands in a cemetery where gravestones of all dates, from 1700 and the years immediately following down to yesterday, may be seen, though most of the stones are so weather-worn that their inscriptions are partially or completely illegible. The oldest gravestone whose inscription remains legible is that of Peter Sandel, died 1708. Of the graves in this ancient yard, however, much the most notable is that of Alexander Wilson, the celebrated ornithologist, who died in 1813. In another section of the city is shown the old school-house in which this distinguished individual at one time taught the youth of the Quaker City.

Of charitable institutions in this section of the city, among the most important are those under the control of the Protestant Episcopal Church, with head-quarters at 411 Spruce Street. This institution, known as the **House of Mercy**, contains the offices of the **City Mission**, and is the location of the **Central Sick-Diet Kitchen**, which has branches in several other sections of the city. These furnish to poor invalids delicate and nutritious food, which would be otherwise beyond their reach. It is also used as a **Home for Consumptives**, which is now supplemented by the spacious home at Chestnut Hill.

Farther south, and in the centre of the poverty-stricken quarter of Philadelphia, is situated the **Bedford Street Mission**, Nos. 619-621 Alaska Street, an institution which has done noble work in improving the unsavory conditions of that locality. Nearer the Delaware several

OLD SWEDES' CHURCH.

institutions devoted to the good of seamen have been established, the principal being the **Seamen's Friend Society**, at 422 South Front Street. This was founded in 1843, and has been of excellent service for the temporal and spiritual good of the sailor. The **Church Home for Seamen of the Port of Philadelphia** is situated at the corner of Swanson and Catharine Streets, in the centre of the shipping trade. At Front and Queen Streets, in the Church of the Redeemer, is a **Seamen's Missionary Association**.

On Catharine Street, above Seventh (Nos. 714-718), is the building of the **Philadelphia Society for the Employment and Instruction of the Poor**, the "Southern House of Industry," an institution which for forty-five years has been actively engaged in good work, giving employment in sewing to about one hundred women, lodging to unemployed men, with meals and baths, schooling to poor children, and performing other charitable labors.

On Washington Avenue, extending to Federal Street, and bounded by Third and Fourth Streets, is **Jefferson Square**, the public breathing-space of this section of the city. It is well-kept and shaded by young and thriving trees. South of this locality, occupying the area bounded by Wolf, Ritner, Fifth, and Sixth Streets, is **Mifflin Square**, one of the new public grounds recently established by the city authorities.

XVI.

NORTH DELAWARE-RIVER FRONT AND VICINITY.

THE river-front, northward from the Willow Street freight-yards, is a scene of almost perpetual business movement upon a large scale. Commercial and manufacturing enterprise has here one of its busiest seats. It is not an attractive quarter of the city in its aspect to the stranger, but thousands of wage-earners here obtain subsistence for their families. Great factories seem to be elbowed by lofty warehouses; extensive lumber-yards are flanked by rolling-mills and foundries; and in many of the poorer streets, too often ill-kept and mean, there are battered and weather-worn, old frame houses, and dingy rows of old-fashioned, low, brick dwellings. This section of the town is a part of the former municipality of the **Northern Liberties**, which, in 1854, was absorbed by Philadelphia. To the north-east lies a section of the town which has its streets running on a plan diverse from that of the principal part of the city, the north and south streets being deflected to the north-east, while those approaching from the west are turned south-eastward. The most densely populated part of this district is called **Kensington**, which may be regarded as being conter-

Kensington. | minous with the Eighteenth Ward, though popular use makes the name a more comprehensive one. We may visit this part of the city either by the Third Street or the Fifth Street horse-cars. The Fifth Street line takes us through a well-built, well-kept, and attractive part of the city, to the vicinity of the Episcopal Hospital (elsewhere noticed), at which point we may begin our walk through this busy, industrial quarter.

The **Episcopal Hospital**, Lehigh Avenue, corner of Front Street, is one of the grandest institutions of the kind in this city. It is a very noble pile of brown-stone buildings, in the Norman style of architecture, and is open to the sick and suffering of every race and creed. The grounds are more than five acres in extent. Founded and first

Episcopal Hospital. | opened in 1852, the hospital was soon found too small for the work it had undertaken. The construction of the present building was undertaken in 1862. In 1862 the first patients were received (wounded Union soldiers, two hundred in number), and in 1874 the building was finished. Situated in a district full of factories and industrial shops, where accidental injuries are frequent, this hospital has always done an excellent work for the poor and suffering of the laboring class. A training-school for nurses is maintained in connection with the Hospital.

South of this locality, at 136 Diamond Street, is the **Kensington Hospital for Women**, an institution organized in 1883 for the treatment of diseases peculiar to women. It is the oldest hospital in the city devoted to this special purpose, is non-sectarian, and depends on charitable contributions for support.

Farther south, near the river, is the traditional locality of Penn's celebrated **Treaty with the Indians**, in 1682. The treaty-elm, under which this agreement is said to have been made, stood till 1810, and the spot (on Beach Street, north of Hanover) is now marked by a small stone monument, erected in 1827. The fact of this treaty having been made lacks historical evidence, and some writers treat it as mythical, but the balance of probabilities seem to be in its favor. The locality of the treaty-monument, long neglected, has recently been made into a public square, and will hereafter be kept in an attractive condition. Kensington possesses two other public pleasure-grounds,—**Norris Square**, at

PENN TREATY MONUMENT.

Howard Street and Susquehanna Avenue, a large and well-shaded tract of ground, and **Fair-Hill Square**, at Fourth Street and Lehigh Avenue, an attractive breathing-place for the neighboring people.

The district of Kensington and those lying to the north of it are notable as being the seat of several of the largest industrial establishments of Philadelphia. Among these, the one at present best known to the general public is the great **Cramp's Ship-Yard**, perhaps the most

Cramp's Ship-Yard.

important establishment of its kind in America. The dry-dock and marine railway of this establishment are on Beach Street, between Ball and Palmer Streets, while the main ship-building yard extends along the river front from Plum to York Streets, covering an extensive tract of ground. The dry-dock and marine railway are among the largest in this country. In the ship-yard have been built several of the largest ships of-war of our new navy, and there are at present five great vessels under way, of from seven thousand five hundred to over ten thousand tonnage and an estimated value of $14,526,000. The five projected huge ocean steamers of the International Steamship Company—companions to the "City of New York" and "City of Paris"—are to be built here, at a cost of $8,000,000 to $9,000,000. This great establishment, which employs in all nearly four thousand hands, has few compeers on either side of the Atlantic.

Among the remaining industrial establishments of the Kensington district there are two worthy of special note for their size and importance. At Hancock and Oxford Streets are located the immense **Keystone Knitting-Mills** of Thomas Dolan & Co., the largest establishment of its kind in America, and with few rivals in the world. On Lehigh Avenue, between Fillmore and Leamy Streets, and extending to Somerset Street, are the great curtain- and rug-mills of **John Bromley & Son**, the most extensive textile-works in the city, if not in the country. The two establishments named cover a great space of ground with their buildings, while the many other large manufacturing concerns in this vicinity make the locality a busy centre of industry.

Keystone Knitting-Mills.

Bromley Mills.

There are some charitable establishments in Kensington worthy of notice, in addition to those already mentioned. On Belgrade Street, above Susquehanna Avenue, is located the **Penn Asylum of Philadelphia**, for indigent widows and single women, established in 1852. This is one of the oldest and worthiest institutions of its kind in the city. At the corner of Frankford Avenue and Palmer Street stands **St. Mary's Hospital**, a large Roman Catholic institution under the charge of conventual ladies of the Franciscan Tertiary Order. Connected with the Hospital is a free dispensary, which is of great service to the poor of this district. At the corner of Lawrence and Huntingdon Streets, opposite Fair-Hill Square, is the **St. Christopher's Hospital for Children**, an active and useful charity.

Penn Asylum.

St. Mary's Hospital.

In this district are two railroad termini, of former importance. At Third and Berks Streets is the passenger station of the North Pennsylvania Railroad, which is now merged into the Reading Railroad system. Two squares east of this is the Kensington Depot of the Pennsylvania Railroad, once the principal terminus of the New York line, but now of minor importance.

Adjoining Kensington on the north is the district known as **Richmond**, that part of it along the river being called **Port Richmond**, and of interest from its extensive exportations of anthracite coal, this being the terminus of the Reading Railroad's coal shipping lines. The great yard here is crossed by a bewildering net-work of tracks, while the many wharves, with their steam colliers taking on cargoes of the "black diamond," are well worthy a visit from strangers. On the river front above the coal wharves stands the **Port Richmond Grain-Elevator**, a lofty structure, visible for miles up and down the river,

PORT RICHMOND COAL WHARVES.

and with a capacity of nine hundred and sixty thousand bushels. Aside from its active industries this district has few attractions. Following the river we come to the districts of Bridesburg and Frankford, in which are some establishments worthy of attention.

The suburb of **Bridesburg**, strictly speaking, is in the Twenty-fifth Ward, lying along the Delaware-River front, and bounded north by the navigable Frankford Creek ; but, popularly, Bridesburg is regarded as extending into the Twenty-third Ward as far as the main line of the Pennsylvania Railroad, on which is **Bridesburg Station**, on Bridge Street, one mile east of Frankford Station. Bridesburg may be reached by the Pennsylvania Railroad or by the Second and Third Street horse-cars. At a short distance south-east of the Pennsylvania Railroad station are the grounds of the **Bridesburg United States Arsenal**, called also the Frankford Arsenal, corner of Tacony Road and Bridge Street, with a considerable frontage on Frankford Creek. Its grounds, more than sixty-two and a half acres in extent, are enclosed by a stone wall and a handsome iron fence. The space within is very finely kept, a large part being well set with trees and shrubs. At present ammunition and tools are manufactured and stored here in magazines; but fire-arms of various kinds have been largely made at this establishment (as was the case during the war of 1861-65); and some large pieces of artillery have occasionally been constructed in the works. This place is well worthy of a visit. It is accessible to visitors at all reasonable hours. Eastward from the Arsenal are the extensive rope and cordage works of **E. H. Fitler & Co.**, one of the largest and finest establishments of the kind in this or any country. Bridesburg proper (south of Frankford Creek) has a considerable number of important manufactories, and is, for the most part, a neatly built and very quiet suburban town.

<small>Bridesburg Arsenal.</small>

The former town of **Frankford**, now included in the Twenty-third Ward, has many of the characteristics of a distinct town. It lies northeast of the Frankford Creek, the lower part of which is navigable, and is the seat of varied and extensive manufactures. Situated five miles north-east of Independence Hall, it is soonest reached by the Pennsylvania Railroad; or, less rapidly, by the horse-cars and dummy-cars of the Fifth and Sixth Street line.

<small>Frankford.</small>

The **Old Ladies' Home of Philadelphia**, formerly located at Frankford Avenue and Clearfield Street, has been removed to Wissanoming, a station on the New York Division of the Pennsylvania Railroad, in this section of the city. It is a non-sectarian institution, conducted on the principle of non-interference with the worship or private life of its inmates, the only requisites being "good moral character, quiet spirit, and peaceful behavior." It is one of the most attractive and comfortable Homes in the city. In this locality are a number of cemeteries. **Greenwood Cemetery**, belonging to the Knights of Pythias, is on Adams Street, or Asylum Turnpike, and to the west of Frankford. Adjoining this on the west is **Mount Auburn Cemetery**. Still farther westward, on the same street, and extending southward to Frankford Creek, are the extensive grounds of the **Friends' Asylum for the Insane**, founded in 1811. It is one of the oldest,

<small>Old Ladies' Home.</small>

<small>Friends' Asylum.</small>

if not the very oldest, insane asylum in the United States. It has a large and commodious, but very plain building. North-eastward from Frankford, on Frankford Avenue (or Bristol Turnpike), and having the Bustleton Turnpike (Bridge Street) on the west, lie **Cedar Hill Cemetery, North Cedar Hill Cemetery,** and **East Cedar Hill Cemetery,** which together form one of the largest burial-grounds within the city limits. They are very neatly laid out, and contain many handsome examples of monumental sculpture.

Two miles north-west of Frankford, on Oxford Road, not far from Fox Chase, is the ancient **Trinity Church** (Episcopalian), which, except Gloria Dei, is the oldest church within the city limits. The present edifice is of brick, and was built in 1714. It may be reached from Ryer's Station, on the Philadelphia, Newtown and New York Railroad.

Tacony, on the river front, two miles north-east of Bridesburg, and on the Pennsylvania Railroad, is another manufacturing suburb, where are located the great **Disston Saw-Works** and other important industrial establishments. The Disston or Keystone Saw-Works are particularly worthy of mention, from their great extent, the army of hands employed, and the fact that they are the largest of their kind in America. Tacony has been in great measure made by those works, and made well, as it would be difficult to find a more attractive collection of workmen's homes, public grounds, and other conveniences, all due to the wise foresight of the Disston Company.

Disston Saw-Works.

Holmesburg, which adjoins Tacony, and forms the Twenty-third Ward of the city, takes its name from Captain Thomas Holmes, Penn's surveyor-general. Near here, and extending along the Pennypack Creek to its junction with the Delaware, is the **House of Correction,** a reformatory institution to which are committed vagrants, drunkards, etc., on complaint and hearing before the municipal magistrates. It includes a tract of over two hundred acres, the buildings consisting of a large main building and a central edifice from which radiate eight extensive wings. The inmates are made to labor in-doors or within the grounds. Near by, on Pennypack Creek, is the location of the new **County Prison.** This has been under construction since 1881, but is not yet finished. It occupies seventeen and a half acres of ground, which are enclosed by a high and strong wall. The buildings consist of a central rotunda and six one-story radiating corridors, with four hundred and forty cells.

House of Correction.

Near Holmesburg is the **Edwin Forrest Home** for retired actors, situated on what was formerly the country-seat of Mr. Forrest, known as "Spring Brook." This estate, together with the bulk of his property, Mr. Forrest bequeathed, by his will, dated April 5, 1866, to his executors, James Oakes, of Boston, James Lawson, of New York, and Daniel Dougherty, of Philadelphia, in trust, for the purposes of this home. The mansion is a roomy old-style structure, three stories high, and has attached to it a farm of one hundred and eleven acres. Busts, portraits, and paintings ornament the interior; there is a library of some eight thousand volumes; an interesting collection of personal belongings of great actors adds its charm; and many of the rooms contain elegant furniture of more than a hundred years of age.

Forrest Home.

Bustleton, the terminus of a branch of the Pennsylvania Railroad (eleven miles out, but within the city limits), is a manufacturing and residential suburb on the Pennypack Creek.

FORREST HOME, HOLMESBURG.

XVII.

Delaware River North and South of the City.

A JOURNEY on the Delaware either above or below the city, by any of the various steamboat lines which ply on this noble stream, will reveal numerous points of attraction in the vicinity of Philadelphia which are worthy of mention. It may be of interest to add to our description of the river front an account of these more remote places. In such a journey not the least attractive feature is the river itself, which expands below the city into one of the widest and most stately streams in this country, while its surface is everywhere enlivened by steam and sailing vessels in great variety.

Going southward, the first place of interest visible on the river-shores is the manufacturing and fishing town of **Gloucester**, on the **Gloucester.** New Jersey side. This has been already mentioned, and it but needs to add that it is the seat of a much-frequented race-course, and has an unsavory reputation as a principal head-quarters of the gambling fraternity. On the opposite side of the river, some distance down-stream, and at the southern extremity of Philadelphia, may be seen the **League Island Navy-Yard**, which merits description. League Island borders the Delaware **League Island Navy-Yard.** shore just above the mouth of the Schuylkill, having a length of two and a quarter miles and a width of a quarter- to a half-mile. It is four miles distant from the City Hall, on the line of Broad Street. This island, having an area of nine hundred and twenty-three acres, was acquired by the United States government in 1876, for navy-yard purposes, its location in fresh water on an easily defensible river, and in the vicinity of the coal- and iron-fields of Pennsylvania, being considered a great advantage. The island has twenty-six feet of water in front, while the Back Channel affords a safe and commodious harbor. Spacious naval and machine buildings and a dry-dock have been constructed, but no work is at present being done, and only some old monitors and the receiving ship St. Louis are stationed here.

Proceeding southward, there become visible, just below the mouth

of the Schuylkill, the low walls of **Fort Mifflin**, a defensive work
guarding the immediate approach to Philadelphia. It

Fort Mifflin. occupies the site of Mud Fort, which in 1777 was built by the patriots to close the river to the British fleet, but
was taken by the British. The work has been reconstructed within
recent years, but is not yet in condition to assail modern war vessels
successfully. Opposite this point, on the Jersey shore, is another
place of historical interest. This is the location known as **Red Bank**,

Red Bank. the site of Fort Mercer of the Revolution, which, on October 21, 1777, repelled an attack by twelve hundred Hessians under Count Donop, who, with three hundred
of his men, was killed. The shape of the ancient intrenchments can
be still made out, while a marble monument commemorates the
event. The government owns a tract of land here, where defensive
works are intended to be built, to supplement Fort Mifflin. Red Bank
has further interest as the site of a large **Sanitarium** for invalid
children, whither numbers of the poor children of Philadelphia are
removed every summer, to breathe the health-giving atmosphere of
the neighboring pine woods.

The next point of interest on the Delaware side is the **Lazaretto**,
the Philadelphia quarantine station, about twelve miles below the
city, and opposite an island with the Indian name of

Lazaretto. **Tinicum**. This station was established in 1806. It
occupies about twelve acres, on which there are several large buildings.
All vessels from foreign ports must stop here for examination by the
quarantine officers between June 1 and October 1, and at other times
if required.

On the New Jersey side of the stream the principal point of interest
south of those named is **Lincoln Park**, a large pleasure-ground, which

Lincoln Park. has become a favorite place of resort during the warm season, being visited by thousands of Philadelphians.
Opposite Tinicum, on the Jersey shore, are the **Dupont
Powder-Works**, whose numerous buildings indicate great activity in
the manufacture of this agent of destruction.

A few miles farther down-stream the city of **Chester** appears in
view, the "Clyde of America," as it has been termed, from the great
ships built at the extensive **Roach Ship-Yard** located here. From the
river numerous other manufacturing establishments are visible, chief
among them being the large **Simpson Print-Works**, at the upper extremity of the city. A few miles below Chester appears the old vil-

lage of **Marcus Hook**, long famous as a gunning and fishing point, its principal products being shad, rail- and reed-birds. Farther down the river nothing of special interest is to be seen until the city of Wilmington is reached, the metropolis of the State of Delaware.

A steamboat journey up the river yields an interest of a different character. The stream steadily narrows, instead of widening, and the flat and monotonous shores of the lower Delaware are replaced by bluff banks, well wooded, and rendered attractive by many suburban towns and handsome water-side country-seats. The first features of interest encountered in a journey in either direction are the islands opposite the centre of the city, which have long obstructed navigation, but are now being removed by monster dredges, most of their material being deposited on League Island. Proceeding up the river, another island, named **Petty's Island**, is soon encountered. This may need to be partly removed for the permanent improvement of the harbor. The places on the Pennsylvania side, within the city limits, have been already described. On the Jersey shore, opposite Richmond, is the well-known **Tammany Fish-House**, and the buildings of various other fishing and boating clubs. Farther up appear in succession the towns known as **Riverton, Riverside, Delanco, Beverly,** and **Edgewater**, while many handsome villas adorn the river-banks. At Riverton is the extensive nursery and seed farm of Henry A. Dreer, of many acres in extent, and among the best in the country. On the Pennsylvania side is visible **Torresdale**, with its numerous beautiful villas, whose verdant lawns run to the water-side, **Andalusia**, and other attractive towns.

At Eddington, a mile and a half above Andalusia, may be seen a structure of much antiquarian interest. This is the modest old building of the club known as the **State in Schuylkill**, the oldest purely social organization in the United States, if not in the world. It was instituted in 1732 as a fishing-club, under the name of Colony in Schuylkill, the present name being adopted after the Revolution. Located for nearly a century at Egglesfield (on the west bank of the Schuylkill River, above Girard Avenue Bridge), it was removed in 1822, on the building of the Fairmount dam, to Rambo's Rock, below the location of the Baltimore and Ohio Railroad bridge; whence, a few years ago, it was taken to its present location, the old castle and kitchen being carefully taken down and rebuilt, the appearance and, as far as possible, the material of the ancient edifice being preserved. The club, whose membership is restricted to twenty-five, now mainly exists as a dining-club, the cooking being done by the members themselves. It possesses many ancient relics, among them two immense pewter platters, presented by a member of the Penn family, and ornamented with the Penn coat of arms.

Farther up-stream, about eighteen miles above the city, appear the large manufacturing towns of **Bristol** on the Pennsylvania and **Burlington** on the New Jersey side of the river. At Bristol begins the great **Landreth Seed Farm**, about six hundred acres of the most fertile land being here devoted solely to the raising of seed. North of Burlington, on the New Jersey side, is the borough of **Bordentown**, notable as the place of residence of Joseph Bonaparte, who settled here after having successively reigned as King of Naples and King of Spain, under the despotic orders of his brother, Napoleon. Opposite is the village of **Tullytown**, above which is **Penn's Manor**, a locality of fine farms, under a high state of culture. Here William Penn resided in 1700 and 1701. The house in which he dwelt no longer remains, it having been taken down before the Revolution. Our journey in this direction ends at the thriving city of **Trenton**, the capital of New Jersey, which is situated at the head of steamboat navigation on the Delaware.

XVIII.

South West-Philadelphia.

This section of West-Philadelphia, which may be said to extend from Market Street, on the north, to the extreme southern limit of Philadelphia is, in the older part, a charming region of well-built homes, of densely shaded and well-paved streets, and of handsome and luxurious churches and useful public institutions. Prominent among the last named is the **University of Pennsylvania**, the most extensive educational establishment in the city or in the State. It occupies commodious grounds, extending from Pine Street to Woodlands Avenue, and running west from Thirty-fourth to Thirty-seventh Street. The main building ("College Hall") is a large and handsome structure of green serpentine stone trimmed with a pale gray-stone. Eastward from this is the highly ornate Library Hall, of redstone and brick, one of the most richly decorated buildings in the city. Its interior is a model of convenience and commodiousness. The library, which contains about one hundred thousand volumes, is especially rich in works on Philology, Political Economy, and American History. In addition the building contains an unusually fine museum of Archaeology and the superb Somerville cabinet of ancient and modern Glyptology, some of whose gems are of almost priceless value. Westward from the College Hall is the Medical Hall, which affords ample accommodations to the medical department of the University,—a department which may be said to give to the University its greatest distinction, and which takes rank with the very foremost medical schools of the land. On Spruce Street, below Thirty-sixth, is the **University Hospital**, an adjunct of the medical department of the University. The main building is a very noble structure of greenstone, in the same general style (called "Collegiate Gothic") as that of the main building of the University. In the rear of the Medical Hall is the Medical and Dental Laboratory (Spruce Street, corner of Thirty-sixth). The **Veterinary College** is near at hand, at the corner of Pine Street and Guardian Avenue. Just west of it is the **Veterinary Hospital**, for sick animals, and still farther west stands the Biological

UNIVERSITY OF PENNSYLVANIA.

Hall of the University. The square of ground between Spruce and Pine and Thirty-sixth and Thirty-seventh Streets is devoted to the athletic sports of the University students. Athletics and physical culture have latterly received special attention in the University. On Thirty-sixth Street, near Pine, is the **Maternity Hospital**, and on Spruce Street, near Thirty-fourth, is the **Nurses' Home**,—both of them adjuncts of the University. The University is reached by the Woodlands Avenue cars of the Market Street line; also by transfers from the other lines of street railways which cross the Schuylkill.

The University of Pennsylvania was first chartered in 1753, as the "Academy and Charitable School of the Province of Pennsylvania,"

VETERINARY DEPARTMENT OF THE UNIVERSITY OF PENNSYLVANIA.

Dr. Franklin being one of the first movers in its establishment. In 1775 its name was changed to "The College and Academy of Philadelphia." In 1779 the University of Pennsylvania was incorporated and invested with the properties and rights of the college; and in 1791 the college and university were united. The Medical School (the oldest in America) was first opened by Dr. William Shippen in 1764. The present main Hospital Buildings of the University were opened in 1874.

In addition to the **College Department**, affiliated with which is the

Towne Scientific School and the Wharton School of Finance, there are departments of Medicine, Dentistry, Veterinary Medicine, Biology, Law, Philosophy, Hygiene, Archaeology and Palaeontology, Physical Education, etc., with a recently added Graduate Department for women.

The **Blockley Almshouse**, so-called, occupies grounds separated by Spruce Street from those of the University of Pennsylvania. It is

Blockley Almshouse. the public refuge or asylum for the pauper class of the town, exclusive of a large number of dependent persons who are cared for in the almost countless private charitable institutions of the city. The Almshouse, with its annexes and adjunct buildings, occupies some one hundred and thirty acres of ground. The buildings are large and commodious, but are more imposing than ornamental in appearance. Connected with it is the **Philadelphia Hospital** (the oldest institution of the kind in the country), with a department for the insane poor. The Almshouse, with the hospitals annexed, accommodates a very large number of the dependent poor. Adjoining the grounds of the Blockley Almshouse, on the south-west, is the **Woodlands Cemetery**, which

Woodlands Cemetery. extends for nearly a mile along Woodlands Avenue (formerly Darby Road) and, on its south-east side, reaches nearly to the River Schuylkill. It covers some eighty acres, and contains a large number of handsome monuments. It is best reached by the Woodlands Avenue horse-cars of the Market Street Railway (Traction Company's lines). This cemetery was formerly included in the estate of "Woodlands," owned at one time by Andrew Hamilton, who was (1701–1703) lieutenant-governor of the province of Pennsylvania. The handsome old residence of the Hamilton family is still standing, in a state of excellent preservation, in the midst of the cemetery grounds.

In the vicinity of the University is another educational institution of leading importance, the recently-opened **Drexel Institute of Art, Science, and Industry**, situated at the north-east corner of Thirty-

Drexel Institute. second and Chestnut Streets. This Institute, whose building was completed in 1891 and opened to the public early in 1892, was founded and endowed by Mr. Anthony J. Drexel, who donated $2,000,000 for this useful purpose. The edifice is an extensive and highly ornamental one, being built of light buff brick with darker terra-cotta ornamental work. Architecturally it is a pure example of the classic Renaissance. It is en-

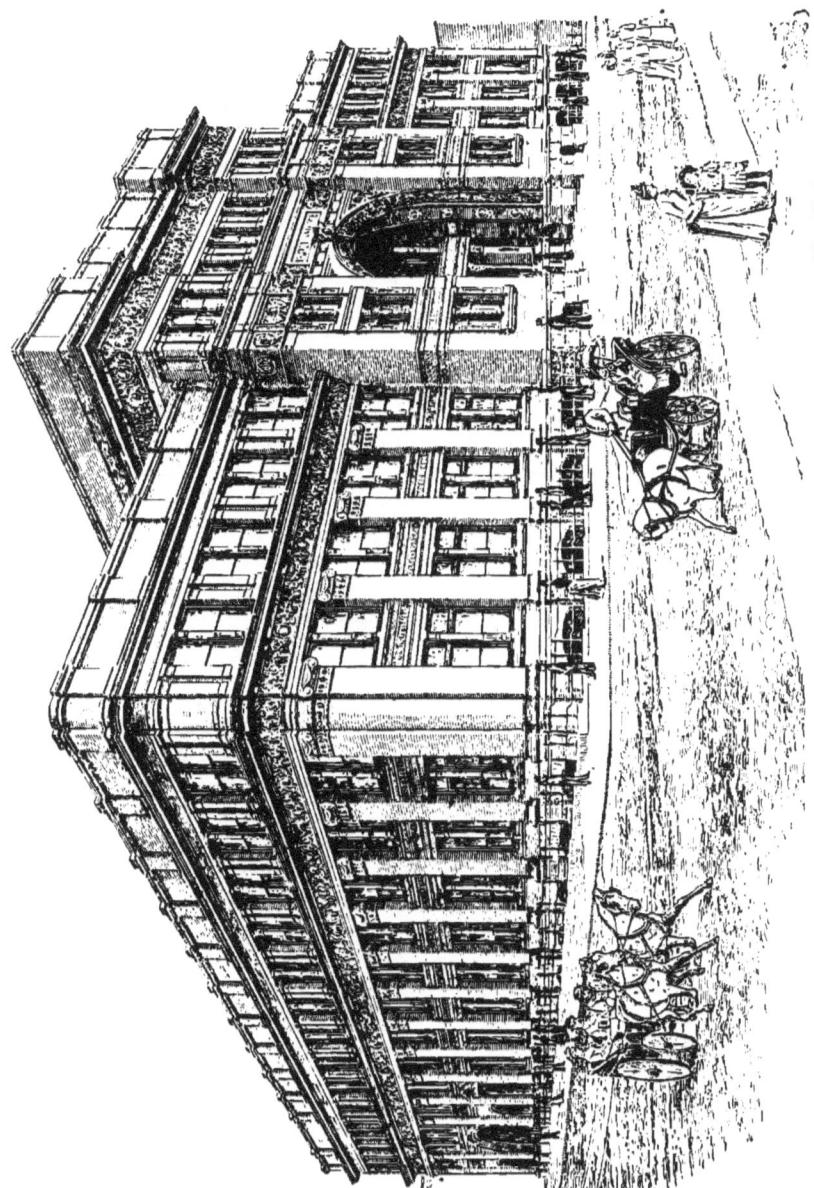

tered by a richly decorated portal on Chestnut Street, which leads to a portico enriched with colored marbles, and thence to a spacious central court, sixty-five feet square and open to the roof, it being covered with a decorated ceiling, with a central area of stained glass. Surrounding this superb court are galleries, enclosed by arcades, and leading to the laboratories, class-rooms, studios, etc., which occupy the upper floors. On the main floor, in addition to the features mentioned, are a library and reading-room, in which is a rare collection of manuscripts presented by Mr. George W. Childs, a museum well supplied with examples of art-work, a lecture-hall with seats for three hundred students, and a large auditorium capable of seating fifteen hundred persons. This Institute is under the charge of Dr. James MacAlister, the well-known recent superintendent of the Philadelphia public schools. The rates of tuition are low, with many free scholarships, and there are departments of art, science, and all the branches of a business and industrial training. The Drexel Institute is one of the most promising of those educational institutions which have adopted recent ideas of physical, industrial, and artistic training, and is unsurpassed by any educational building in the world in appointments, laboratory facilities, and the architectural beauty and general adaptation to its purpose of the edifice.

A short distance north-east of the Drexel Institute, on Market Street, west of the Market Street Bridge, is the newly-built **Philadelphia Market,** an extensive and excellently-appointed structure, under

Philadelphia Market.

the auspices of the Pennsylvania Railroad, whose tracks deliver supplies directly to the building. Its business is chiefly wholesale, it being in effect a Farmers' Wholesale Market.

If now we pass to the more remote portions of this section of the city, we find ourselves in a region filled with attractive residences, many of them of great beauty, and the seat of numbers of fine churches and useful charitable institutions, of which the more notable merit description.

The **Tabernacle Presbyterian Church,** corner of Thirty-seventh and Chestnut Streets, is one of the finest American examples of the

Tabernacle Presbyterian Church.

English decorated Gothic architecture. The view on the Thirty-seventh Street side, including the chapel gate, the cloistered walk, and the manse, is especially effective. The body of this noble pile is of Potomac granite, with elaborate and beautiful windows set in carved Indiana limestone. The interior is finished in solid oak, and is richly adorned with ecclesiastical symbols, the whole forming one of the most impressive and beautiful church interiors in the United States.

The Roman Catholic **Church of St. James the Greater**, at Thirty-eighth and Chestnut Streets, is one of the most elaborate in the country. It is built of Baltimore marble, with granite foundations. It is of Gothic architecture, with a clear-story, and the external effect is extremely fine; while the interior is especially beautiful and impressive. The high altar is considered, by critics, the handsomest work of its kind in the United States. The district of South West-Philadelphia contains numerous other churches, many of them of striking and effective architecture. In addition to those described, however, we have space only to speak of the very imposing **Christ Memorial Church** (Reformed Episcopal), at Chestnut and Forty-third Streets, which, with its adjacent Divinity School, forms a noble architectural landmark. The whole group of buildings is of Indiana and Avondale limestone, and affords an excellent example of the English decorated Gothic style.

Of the charitable institutions we can speak only of those of leading importance. The **Indigent Widows' and Single Women's Asylum** occupies a beautiful quadrangle of buildings on Chestnut Street near Thirty-seventh. This Asylum was founded in 1819 by Miss Rawson, and is managed by a society of ladies. The institution is strictly non-sectarian, but religious services are regularly sustained by clergymen of various denominations.

At the north-east corner of Forty-fifth Street and Osage Avenue, south of Pine Street, is the **Home of the Merciful Saviour for Crippled Children**, a very deserving and praiseworthy charity. Crippled children are received without entrance fee, and are supported by the voluntary gifts of the friends of the institution. This Home is under Episcopalian supervision, but is non-sectarian in spirit and methods. The **Home for Destitute Colored Children**, Woodlands Avenue near Forty-sixth Street, combines a simple and rudimentary course of schooling and a measure of industrial training, preparatory to a life of usefulness. At a suitable age the children are indentured, chiefly with families resident in the country. At the corner of Forty-eighth Street and Woodlands Avenue are seen the extensive and ornate buildings of the **Philadelphia Home for Incurables**, one of the most interesting and important of the many estimable charities of this city of brotherly love. The Home is entirely undenominational, and its management is largely in the hands of ladies. Nearly all its officers and managers are ladies, but a number of gentlemen are chosen annually to fill the advisory boards. The Home was organized and incorporated in 1877. Its buildings and grounds occupy about five acres. The **Educational Home**, at Forty-eighth Street and Greenway Avenue, is at present occupied as a home and school for Indian boys, under the care of the Protestant Episcopal Church. It occupies a plain and commodious building. The boys learn certain industrial pursuits. The progress here made by the young Indians seems to be in every way encouraging to the friends of the recent movement to reclaim and rescue the remnant of the aboriginal race in this country.

The Protestant Episcopal **Divinity School**, at Fifty-first Street and

Episcopal Div. School. Woodlands Avenue, is a handsome structure of dark gray-stone, finished with brick, in an ornate Gothic style. Near it stands a handsome chapel and other buildings belonging to the School. The **Presbyterian Home for Widows and Single Women** is near Fifty-eighth Street and Greenway Avenue

Presbyterian Home. (near Woodlands Avenue), and may be reached either by the Darby street-cars, or by the Baltimore and Ohio Railroad, Fifty-eighth Street Station. The building is a large and imposing structure of stone, and accommodates a great number of old ladies. One square to the north-west (corner of Fifty-eighth Street and Kingsessing Avenue) is the **Presbyterian Orphanage**, which occupies four large stone cottages, with other buildings, among which is a stone chapel of beautiful proportions. This is an extremely useful and effective charity.

One of the curiosities of south-western Philadelphia is the ancient

Kingsessing Church. **St. James's Church, Kingsessing**, on Woodlands Avenue near Sixty-eighth Street. It is one of the "Old Swedish" Lutheran Churches which early became Episcopalian, as it is at present. The present church edifice was built of stone, in 1763, and has since been enlarged. It is interesting as a specimen of the American architecture of the colonial times. "Kingsessing," the name of this district, is properly the name of one of the old townships now merged in Philadelphia. At Seventieth Street and Woodlands Avenue is the **House of the Guardian Angel and Maternity Hospital**, of the Roman Catholic Church, chiefly devoted to the care of young infants. This section of the city is often called

Paschal, or Paschalville. It is quickly reached either by the Baltimore and Ohio or the Philadelphia, Wilmington, and Baltimore Railroads.

Angora, on the Central Division, Philadelphia, Wilmington, and Baltimore Railroad (four and one-half miles out), is a neat suburb in the Twenty-seventh Ward. Directly at the station is the **Church Home for Children**, a handsome and spacious building of green-stone. On the same grounds is a tasteful chapel of stone. The Home was opened in 1873. On the same street (Fifty-eighth), a short distance south of the railway, is the **Baptist Orphanage**, which occupies four large and beautiful cottages of brick, grouped together on a wide and roomy lawn. This is one of the best-managed of the many Philadelphia Homes for orphans.

XIX.

North West-Philadelphia.

THAT part of West Philadelphia which lies north of Market Street and south of the Zoological Gardens embraces within its limits a beautiful quarter of the city, portions of it being densely shaded with trees, and the principal streets being lined with very fine houses, for the most part surrounded by lawns and shrubbery. Churches and benevolent institutions abound also in this part, as in other sections, and numerous lines of street-cars, running in various directions, render all parts easily accessible.

We shall confine ourselves to a description of the leading charitable institutions, many of which are attractively located and have large and excellently-adapted buildings. At No. 3518 Lancaster Avenue is the **Working Home for Blind Men**, one of the worthiest institutions of the kind in this city. It occupies extensive buildings, has more than one hundred and twenty inmates, and is nearly self-supporting. Near by, at No. 3524 Lancaster Avenue, is the **Pennsylvania Retreat for Blind Mutes and Aged and Infirm Blind Persons**, "a charity so peculiar that its very name is a touching appeal." North of this location, at Thirty-fifth Street and Fairmount Avenue, is the **House of the Good Shepherd** (Roman Catholic), an abode and reformatory for abandoned women of every race and creed; there is also connected with it a reformatory for intemperate women. This has proved an extremely useful institution.

The **Old Man's Home**, on Powelton Avenue, extending westward from Saunders Avenue, occupies a large gray-stone building with supplementary buildings. It is surrounded by well-shaded grounds, and affords a comfortable shelter for its aged inmates. Directly opposite, occupying a large square of ground between Powelton Avenue and Filbert Street, and extending from Saunders Avenue to Thirty-ninth Street, is the **Presbyterian Hospital**, which is one of the best institutions of its kind in the city. The buildings comprise six commodious brick pavilions, used as hospital wards, and a central administration building, which, with two of the wards, was added in January, 1891. The administration building is a handsome edifice, of brick, terra-cotta, and stone, six stories high and forty-five by one hundred and eight feet in ground area. This Hospital, which is now in its twenty-second year, has considerably increased its endowment fund and extended its range of usefulness within recent years. It has a large number of free beds, with excellent accommodations for private patients. During the year 1891 nearly nine hundred patients were treated in its wards, and a much larger number in its out-patient department. Very near to the above two institutions, at the north-east corner of Saunders and Powelton Avenues, is the **Pennsylvania Industrial Home for Blind Women**, a handsome brick edifice with a commodious annex of stone. Farther west, at Forty-first and Baring Streets, is the **Western Home for Poor Children**, whose large and comfortable building is situated on spacious and well-kept grounds. At the corner of Belmont and Girard Avenues stands the **Home for Aged and Infirm Colored Persons**. This institution is supported largely by members of the Society of Friends. It occupies a spacious and comfortable stone building, with attractive grounds. Another useful institution in this vicinity is the **Western Temporary Home**, which embraces also a **Home for Convalescents**, situated at No. 35 North Fortieth Street. With it are connected a day nursery and a sick-diet kitchen.

The large tract of ground lying north of Market Street, south of Haverford Avenue, west of Forty-second Street, and east of Forty-ninth Street is occupied by the **Pennsylvania Hospital for the Insane** (commonly known as Kirkbride's Hospital). There are

Kirkbride's Hospital.

separate groups of buildings for the two sexes. The hospital-buildings are large and commodious, and are handsomely built of stone. The grounds (about one hundred and eleven acres) are handsomely laid out as pleasure-grounds, but a part is cultivated as a farm. The Market Street cars pass directly by the grounds. This institution is, strictly speaking, a branch of the Pennsylvania Hospital, elsewhere noticed. Like the parent hospital from which it branched off in 1841, it is supported entirely by private contributions, bequests, and fees from patients, there being a certain number of freebeds maintained for the indigent insane. Nearly opposite to the main entrance to Kirkbride's, but some three squares to the north, at No. 4618 Westminster Avenue, is the **Philadelphia Home for Infants**, a non-sectarian institution, founded in 1873. Many of the infants here cared for are admitted and boarded without charge; for others a nominal fee is paid.

A mile or more west from Kirkbride's Hospital, extending to the extreme limit of the city, and reached by extensions of the Traction Company's Market Street line, is the suburb of Haddington, a locality of few present attractions, but improving from year to year. **The Home for Aged Couples of the Presbyterian Church** occupies modest but very comfortable quarters at Sixty-fifth and Vine Streets. Here old and indigent married couples of the Presbyterian faith are well cared for, a moderate fee being required on their admission. This Home was opened in 1885.

Haddington.

At Sixty-fourth Street and Lansdowne Avenue, on a commanding elevation, stand the commodious and beautiful stone buildings of the **Philadelphia Orphan Asylum,** one of the best of Philadelphia's public charities. The ample grounds are kept in the most tasteful order, and the numerous children here sustained and schooled have the best of care. The orphans are all, or nearly all, children of the pauper class; but brighter or happier-looking children it would be hard to find anywhere.

The **Burd Orphan Asylum,** on Market Street, beyond Sixty-third Street, stands in Delaware County, just beyond the county line (which here follows a small stream called Cobb's Creek). The situation is very beautiful. The grounds have an extent of forty-five acres, and the buildings are of gray-stone, in a plain but graceful English Gothic style. The asylum is for white female orphans of the Protestant Episcopal Church, and is under the management of the rector and members of St. Stephen's Church, Tenth Street below Market. It was founded in 1848 by Eliza H. Burd, widow of Edward Shippen Burd; the present building was opened in 1863.

Burd Orphan Asylum.

North-eastward from Haddington is the ancient suburb of **Hestonville,** reached from the city by the Arch Street, and by the Race and Vine Street horse-cars, or by the Pennsylvania Railroad (Fifty-second Street station). Hestonville has an antiquated appearance, and abounds in curious oldish houses of the style, or styles, of fifty years ago; but the hand of improvement has touched it, and all will soon be renovated. In fact, for many years, some streets in its vicinity have been occupied by comfortable, and even luxurious abodes, some of them of the best class. The visitor approaching Hestonville by horse-car sees to the left the extensive **Cathedral Cemetery** (Forty-eighth to Fifty-second Street), between Girard and Wyalusing Avenues; on the north side,

Hestonville.

partly enclosed by the cemetery, is a large Roman Catholic church, dedicated to **Our Mother of Sorrows**. It has a heavy and sombre appearance, quite in keeping with its name and surroundings.

Returning from these extreme western limits of the city to the vicinity of the Schuylkill, we find a markedly different state of affairs. The quiet and tasteful residence aspect of the section just left is replaced by the busiest of railroad scenes, the space above Market Street from the river to Thirty-second Street being occupied by the train-yards of the Pennsylvania Railroad, which are covered with a net-work of tracks, and present a scene of activity by day and night which is well worthy of observation. Near Market Street Bridge is a large freight warehouse, just north of which are long lines of cattle-sheds, the lanes between them threaded by tracks for the convenience of cattle-trains. North of these, again, is a large **Abattoir**, in which numbers of cattle and other food animals daily meet their death for the supply of the Philadelphia markets. Various other buildings occupy the grounds, among them those of the **Powelton Avenue Station** for West-Philadelphia, at which nearly all trains stop. Standing on the elevated Spring Garden Street Bridge, a scene of incessant activity is visible,—swift-darting passenger- or lumbering freight-trains passing almost momentarily under our feet, partly west-bound, over the **Main Line**, partly following the tracks of the **New York Division** and skirting the Zoological Gardens, which we shall next describe.

The famous **Zoological Garden**, on the west bank of the Schuylkill River, and bounded by Girard Avenue, is one of the most attractive features not only of this section, but of the city. It occupies a tract formerly the country-seat of John Penn, grandson of the founder, and known as "Solitude." The house built by Penn still stands in the grounds. The tract contains thirty-three acres, and is, in fact, part of Fairmount Park, the commissioners of which lease it to the Zoological Society of Philadelphia, who have established here the most successful collection of animals existing in America. The buildings are tasteful, picturesque, and suitable to their purposes, and are set in grounds beautifully planted and kept. It is a most interesting and instructive place to visit, and is a favorite resort of children, citizens, and sojourners in the city. No expense has been spared in procuring animals or fitting up the garden in the manner best adapted to their maintenance and exhibition. The society has agents in every part of the world constantly on the alert for rare and interesting specimens of natural history. The collection includes a large representation of American fauna. The shaggy-coated buffalo, the lordly elk and timid deer, wolves, raccoons, foxes, prairie-dogs, rattlesnakes, bears, water-fowl, sea-lions, and specimens of nearly every other beast, bird, or reptile that belongs to the continent are here found under conditions making it easy and pleasant to observe their appearance and habits. Besides these, South America, India, Africa,

BEAR-PITS. ZOOLOGICAL GARDEN.

and the islands of the sea contribute their portion to the collection. Elephants, camels, lions and tigers, the ugly rhinoceros, sportive monkeys and the anthropoid apes, great serpents, and beautifully-plumaged birds swell the list of attractions, which can here be only hinted at.

This collection is the only one in this country which at all approaches in completeness and fitness of bestowal the great zoological garden in Regent's Park, London, or the Jardin d'Acclimatation of Paris. The expenses of its maintenance are very large, and the society has at times been hard pressed in keeping it up to the high standard which it has attained. Considerable sums by way of endowment have been subscribed by liberal citizens, and it is to be hoped that the example thus set may be emulated by others.

Near the Girard Avenue entrance to the Garden is the bronze group, by Wilhelm Wolf, called "The Dying Lioness," which is re-

THE DYING LIONESS.

garded by critics as one of the most effective pieces of animal sculpture to be seen in this country. Frequent trains on the Pennsylvania Railroad, running from Broad Street Station, stop at the Zoological Garden, besides which an extension of the Lombard and South Streets line of horse-cars, starting from Twenty-fifth and South Streets, convey passengers to this point, and the Girard Avenue cars pass the main entrance.

XX.

FAIRMOUNT WATER-WORKS AND VICINITY.

Two miles north-west of the City Hall, on the east bank of the Schuylkill River, and approached by way of the Arch Street cars, the Vine Street and Callowhill Street lines, the Girard Avenue line, and the Fairmount branches of the Spruce and Pine and Traction lines, are the famous Fairmount Water-Works, to which, since their

GRAFF MONUMENT.

small beginnings, more than half a century ago, the city of Philadelphia has been, in a large measure, indebted for so much of its water-supply as came from the Schuylkill River. Here, near the close of the first quarter of the present century, under the superintendence of

Frederick Graff, the designer and first engineer of the water-works (and whose services are commemorated by a monument on the grounds), was begun that system of water-supply which, since carried on through successive stages of development, now yields to the city, on an average, the enormous quantity of over 105,000,000 gallons of water per day.

The beginning of the now immense Fairmount Park was the comparatively small tract which is immediately appurtenant to these water-works, which date from 1822, though the city was, through other channels, first supplied with water from the Schuylkill in 1790. Enormous engines, worked by water-power, force water from the river to the top of the hill,—the original "Fair-Mount,"—where it is held in a distributing reservoir. From the top of this reservoir, ninety-five feet above the level of the river, a charming prospect is presented to the beholder, embracing in a semi-birds-eye view numberless attractive features, near and remote, with which the city abounds. Passing the base of the hill runs the Schuylkill River, spanned here and there by several bridges, while beyond, on the vast net-work of tracks of the Pennsylvania Railroad, is an almost unceasing succession of moving trains. West Philadelphia, with its semi-rural features, adds a pleasing variety to the landscape, contrasting strikingly with the densely built-up portions of the city. Far down the river on the right are seen the fine buildings of the University of Pennsylvania, while on the left the Naval Asylum and the Schuylkill Arsenal are conspicuous. Hundreds of tall steeples and massive towers rise into view in all directions, among which the beholder will readily distinguish the striking group composed of the towers of the new City Hall and its surrounding buildings, at Broad and Market Streets, The station of the Baltimore and Ohio Railroad, at Twenty-fourth and Chestnut Streets; the Church of the Holy Trinity, at Nineteenth and Walnut Streets; the dome of the Cathedral, on Logan Square; the tower of the beautiful Catholic High School, at Broad and Vine Streets; and the spire of the beautiful Mary J. Drexel Home, near Girard College, are striking features in the remoter landscape.

More immediately the view from the Reservoir hill takes in two of the handsomest streets of the city, Spring Garden Street, whose wide and smooth expanse presents an animated scene, from the great number of carriages and bicycles which make it their avenue of approach to the Park, and Green Street, narrower in width, but attrac-

GREEN STREET ENTRANCE TO FAIRMOUNT PARK.

tive from its numerous handsome residences, each with its plot of greensward in front.

South of these streets is a locality busy with industry, a large number of manufacturing establishments, for the production of textile and iron goods, soaps, shoes, zephyrs, braids, and various other articles, being clustered in this vicinity. As these establishments are near this portion of the Park, the most prominent of them may be noted here. On Pennsylvania Avenue, extending from Twenty-first to Twenty-second Street, with warehouse and office on Spring Garden Street, are the extensive **Pequea Mills** of William Wood & Co., one of the largest cotton- and woollen-mills in the city. Near this establishment, on Callowhill Street, between Twentieth and Twenty-first Streets, is the large machine-tool manufactory of **Bement, Miles & Co.**, its only rival in the city being the similar works of William Sellers & Co., already mentioned. Other large establishments are the **Fairmount Machine-Works**, the **Caledonian Carpet-Works**, the **McKeone Soap-Works**, the **Erben, Search & Co. Zephyr-Works**, and the **Star Braid-Works**, each of importance in its special line.

<small>Pequea Mills</small>

<small>Bement, Miles & Co.</small>

The principal entrance to this part of the East Park is from Green Street, where, on his left, the visitor has the above-named reservoir, the buildings pertaining to the water-works, and the steamboat-landing. Next, crossing an open space ornamented with a handsome bronze statue of Lincoln, erected by the Lincoln Monument Association in the fall of 1871, we come to a hill covered with trees, among which go winding paths, and under which green grass and flowering shrubs combine their attractions, while around its base flowers bloom and fountains play, and the curving drive displays an almost unbroken line of carriages. This is Lemon Hill, and on its summit is the mansion in which Robert Morris had his home during the Revolutionary struggle. Here the great financier loved to dwell. Here he entertained many men whose names were made illustrious by those stirring times. Between this historic mansion, which now plays the humble part of a restaurant, and the brow of the hill is the attractive amphitheatre where free open-air concerts are given in the summer. There are seats here for more than three thousand people, and the locality is one of the most beautiful in the Park, with its semicircular arcade, its verdant terraces, its numerous trees, and its winding paths. A short distance above stands the Lemon Hill Observatory,

a tall skeleton tower of iron, erected in the Centennial year, and still used by those who wish to obtain an extensive view of city and country.

At the foot of Lemon Hill, nestled on the bank of the river, are the handsome houses of the boating clubs, built of stone and generally in a Gothic style of architecture. These clubs, numbering a dozen or more, with an aggregate membership of about fifteen hundred, constitute the Schuylkill Navy, and form the germ of the Athletic Club of the Schuylkill Navy, whose beautiful club-house, at Nos. 1626-28 Arch Street, is one of the most attractive features of that section of the city.

Following the carriage-drive, we arrive at **Grant's Cottage**, a small building of upright hewn logs, which was used by General Grant as his head-quarters at City Point, Virginia, and was brought here after the close of the war. Near by, the Girard Avenue Bridge crosses the Schuylkill, under which bridge passes the very pleasant river-drive of the East Park. A large statue of Alexander von Humboldt, presented to Philadelphia by her German citizens, overlooks the Girard Avenue entrance. About midway between this and the Lincoln monument there is an excellent statue of the late Hon. Morton McMichael.

<small>Grant's Cottage.</small>

This section of the Park is adorned with various other works of art, the gift of the Fairmount Park Art Association. The most interesting of these are the bronze statue of a "Lioness bringing Food to her Young," by Auguste Cain, in the flower-bed at the south end of Lemon Hill; the sandstone "Tam O'Shanter" group, with its humorous significance, on the west flank of the same hill, the work of the Scotch artist Thom; and the artistic equestrian statue of "Joan of Arc," by Fremiet, at the Girard Avenue end of the drive, perhaps the finest example of French bronze statuary in this country. The remainder of the Park contains various other attractive examples of statuary, purchased and presented by the energetic association above named.

XXI.

East Fairmount Park and Vicinity.

The territory included in Fairmount Park was formerly taken up with gentlemen's estates, which, from a very early date, crowned with their mansions its commanding heights, and covered with their pleasure-grounds its wooded slopes and lovely vales. Several of the old-time colonial mansions are still preserved within the precincts of the Park, and are fraught with associations that make them precious souvenirs of by-gone days. Adjoining, on the north, the section embraced in the immediate environs of the Fairmount Water-Works is the division of this great pleasure-ground commonly recognized as the **East Park**, extending in an almost continuous tract from Girard Avenue to the Wissahickon, and including within its limits miles of charming walks and carriage-drives, besides many objects of interest relating to old-time and modern Philadelphia.

Just beyond the Girard Avenue Bridge is the Connecting Railroad Bridge, as it is popularly termed, which unites the Pennsylvania Railroad with its New York Division. Through the rocky bluff which forms the eastern abutment of the bridge a short tunnel has been cut for a carriage road. This route was opened in the summer of 1871, and developed some of the loveliest scenery in all the Park. A number of fine old country-seats were absorbed in this portion of the grounds, and they remain very nearly as their former owners left them. The **Spring Garden Water-Works**, with a pumping capacity of considerably over one hundred million gallons daily, which will soon

Spring Garden Water-Works.

be increased to over one hundred and fifty millions, are situated just north of Girard Avenue, and are well worthy a visit, their great Worthington and other steam-pumps being objects of much interest, while the buildings and their surroundings are attractive features of the locality. The densely-built portion of the city which borders this section of the Park is often called "Brewery-town," from the great number of breweries here established. Principal among these is the extensive **Bergner & Engel**

East Park Reservoir.

establishment, the largest of its kind in the city. Northward from this locality is the great **East Park Reservoir** (supplied by the Spring Garden works), which covers an area of one hundred and six acres and has a storage capacity of over seven hundred million gallons. Aside from its utility, it has been so treated as to make it an attractive feature of the landscape.

Adjoining the upper extremity of this reservoir is **Mount Pleasant**, the former residence of Benedict Arnold. It was built about 1762,

SCHUYLKILL FALLS BLUFFS, BELOW EDGELY.

and was purchased by Arnold as a marriage-gift for his wife in 1779.

Mount Pleasant.
It is now reduced to the humble office of a Park dairy. West of this mansion is **Rockland**, built about 1810, and situated in a very picturesque portion of the Park. A short distance above the mansion is a jutting point or promontory from which may be had a beautiful view of the river and of the heights beyond.

North from Mount Pleasant is **Ormiston**, beyond which lies **Edgely**, both old estates, while still farther north is **Strawberry Mansion**, occu-

Strawberry Mansion.
pying the summit of a lofty elevation, with a steep and rocky face to the river, up which has been constructed a foot-path, which, with its arched portal, stone steps, and rustic balustrade, is a picturesque feature of the river-drive. The grounds about Strawberry Mansion are handsomely decorated.

THE WALK TO STRAWBERRY MANSION.

Daily open-air concerts are given here in the summer. Beyond Strawberry Hill the road skirts the river at the foot of Laurel Hill Cemetery, traverses the front of Falls of Schuylkill village, and brings us to the bridge which here serves as a connecting link between the East and West Parks.

XXII.

WEST FAIRMOUNT PARK AND VICINITY

By far the largest part of the Park, exclusive of that narrow strip which borders the Wissahickon, lies west of the Schuylkill River, the extreme south-east angle being occupied by the Zoological Garden. The various sections of the tract are conveniently reached by the

LANSDOWNE DRIVE.

Girard Avenue horse-cars, which enter it over the fine Girard Avenue Bridge; by the trains of the Pennsylvania Railroad, from Broad Street Station, which stop at the Zoological Garden and at Park Station on the Schuylkill Valley Division, and by the trains of the Reading (Main Line) and of the Baltimore and Ohio Railroads, which stop at Girard Avenue Station. The Chestnut and Walnut, the Market, the Arch Street, the Girard Avenue, and other lines of cars also run to the West Park.

Carriages enter the West Park over the Girard Avenue Bridge by way of the Lansdowne drive, which winds through what was formerly the picturesque estate of Lansdowne, owned by John Penn, "the American," whose nephew, also named John, built here a stately

SWEET BRIER FROM EGGLESFIELD.

mansion, known as Egglesfield, in which he lived during the Revolutionary war. Just after entering the Lansdowne drive we pass, on our left, the Penn (or Letitia) House, which has, on account of its great historical interest, been removed to this point from its old location in Letitia Street. It was built in 1682-83, was the first brick building in Philadelphia, and is the oldest building now standing in Pennsylvania. It served as the State House of the Province for many years, the governor and the colonial assembly meeting here frequently. It will probably stand in its present location for centuries, as a memento of the birthday of this section of our country.

Sweet Brier mansion is the next passed, from which point there is a lovely view of the river above, and then, crossing the ravine by a rustic bridge, we are in a section of the Park which was the scene of **Horticultural Hall.** the great Centennial Exhibition of 1876. Of the Exhibition buildings only two now remain, **Horticultural Hall** and Memorial Hall. The site of the former was most happily chosen. It occupies a bluff that overlooks the Schuylkill one hundred feet to the eastward, and is bounded by the deep

VIEW ABOVE SWEET BRIER.

channels of a pair of brooks equidistant on the north and south sides. Up the banks of these clamber the sturdy arboreal natives, as though to shelter in warm embrace their delicate kindred from abroad. Broad walks and terraces prevent their too close approach and the consequent exclusion of sunlight.

Entering from the side by a neat flight of steps in dark marble, we find ourselves in a gayly-tiled vestibule thirty feet square, between forcing-houses, each one hundred by thirty feet. Advancing, we enter the great conservatory, two hundred and thirty by eighty feet, and fifty-five high, much the largest in this country, and but a trifle inferior in height to the palm-houses of Chatsworth and Kew. A gallery twenty feet from the floor carries us up among the dates and cocoanuts. The decorations of this hall are in keeping with the external design. The dimensions of the building are three hundred and eighty by one hundred and ninety-three feet.

Outside promenades, four in number, and each one hundred feet long, lead along the roofs of the forcing-houses, and contribute to the portfolio of lovely views that enriches the Park. Other prospects are offered by the upper floors of the east and west fronts, the aërial terrace embracing in all seventeen thousand square feet. Restaurants, reception-rooms, and offices occupy the two ends. The cost of the building was $251,937.

Leaving Horticultural Hall, we cross the bridge spanning the picturesque Lansdowne Ravine to **Memorial Hall**, which, as its name

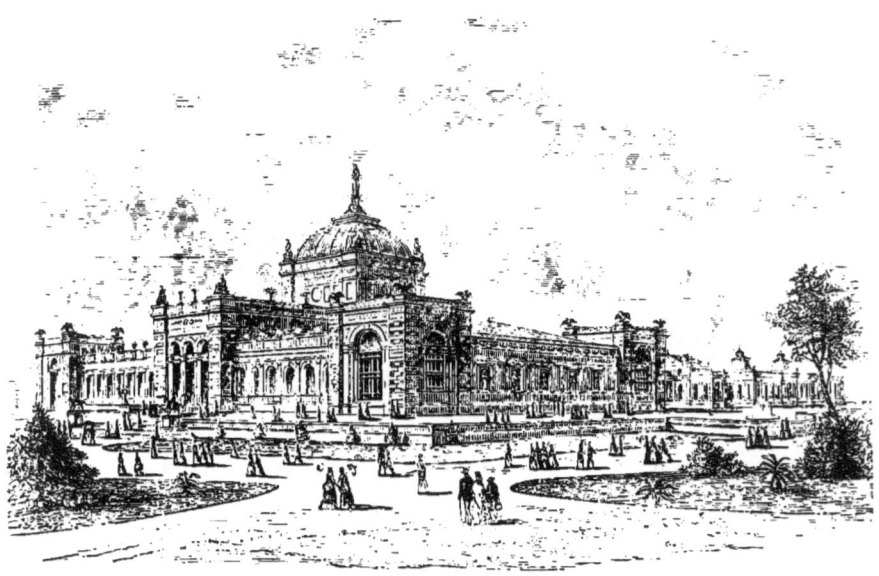

MEMORIAL HALL.

implies, contemplates indefinite durability. What Virginia and Massachusetts granite, in alliance with Pennsylvania iron, on a basis of one

Memorial Hall. million five hundred thousand dollars, can effect in that direction, seems to have been done. The façade is in ultra-Renaissance, with arch and balustrade and open arcade. The square central tower, or what under a circular dome would be the drum, is quite in harmony with the main front in proportion and outline, and renders the unity of the building very striking. That its object, of supplying the best light for pictures and statuary, is not lost sight of, is evidenced by the fact that three-fourths of the interior space is lighted from above, and the residue has an ample supply from lofty windows.

Memorial Hall is of particular interest from the great collection of objects of Industrial Art, belonging to the school of that name, here displayed; its several large groups of works of fine and useful art on special exhibition; the Great Rothermel painting of the "Battle of Gettysburg," the property of the State; and numerous other objects of interest. Here will soon be placed the costly Wilstach collection of paintings, recently donated to the city, which should make the Hall a place of pilgrimage for lovers of the fine arts, and may serve as a nucleus for future similar donations, and, with the above-named collections, form the foundation of a great gallery of the fine and the useful arts.

From the Exhibition grounds we may take our way to **George's Hill**, up whose rather steep ascent we wind until at the summit we have attained an elevation of two hundred and ten feet above high

George's Hill. tide. This tract, containing eighty-three acres, was presented to the city by Jesse and Rebecca George, whose ancestors had held it for many generations. As a memorial of their generosity, this spot was named George's Hill, and its rare advantages of scenery and location will keep their name fresh forever. It is the grand objective-point of pleasure-parties. Few carriages make the tour of the Park without taking George's Hill in their way, and stopping for a few moments on its summit to rest their horses and let the inmates feast their eyes on the view which lies before them,—a view bounded only by League Island and the Delaware.

At the foot of George's Hill, on the side next to the city, is an elaborate allegorical fountain, adorned with marble statues, erected at the time of the Centennial Exhibition by the Catholic Total Abstihence Union, and on the top of the Hill is **Belmont Reservoir**, with a storage capacity of forty million gallons, from which West-Philadelphia receives its principal water-supply, the water being pumped from the Schuylkill River by the Belmont Water-Works, located near the Reading Railroad bridge over the Schuylkill. About a mile northward from George's Hill, on a sightly location in the Park (easily reached even by pedestrians), is **Belmont Mansion**, now a house of entertainment for callers, but once the home of the celebrated Peters family of ante-Revolutionary fame. The original dwelling, a portion of which is still standing, was erected before the middle of the last century, and to this large additions were subsequently made. The eminent Judge Richard Peters, scholar, wit, and patriot,

CATHOLIC TOTAL ABSTINENCE UNION FOUNTAIN.

was born and died here (1744-1828), and here, while enjoying the hospitality of Judge Peters, Washington is said to have planted a Spanish walnut-tree, which grew to large size, and Lafayette, in 1824, planted a white walnut.

The view from the piazza of the house is one which can scarcely be surpassed in America. It is one of those grand effects of nature and art combined, which man must acknowledge his inability to represent adequately on paper.

On the river front, below Belmont, is the rustic house said to have been the residence of the poet Tom Moore while in this country, though this is problematical. Between it and Belmont winds up a deeply shaded and most romantic walk, known as Belmont Glen, a favorite stroll for lovers of the picturesque. North of this stretches a wide expanse of woodland, with many attractive nooks and defiles, in a secluded corner of which is located the **Park Nursery**. The carriage road from Belmont passes along the brow of the hill, **Belmont Driving Park**, a much-frequented race-course, lying a short distance westward. From the drive a magnificent view of the East Park and the course of the Schuylkill is gained, the special features of the landscape being the monumental wealth of Laurel Hill Cemetery, just beyond, and the roofs and spires of the hill-inclosed town of Manayunk, closing the view to the northward. Reaching **Chamouni**, an old mansion with a lake and concourse, and a thickly-wooded dale to the west, the northern limit of the West Park is attained, a bridge here crossing the Schuylkill to the East Park at Falls Village.

XXIII.

LAUREL HILL CEMETERY AND BEYOND.

Laurel Hill Cemetery. LAUREL HILL is one of the oldest and most celebrated of American suburban cemeteries, having been opened for burials in 1825. Its natural site was always one of great beauty; and its charms have been vastly improved by the skill of the landscape gardener and the lavish hand of wealth. It is pre-eminent for the elegance and variety of its monumental work and mortuary sculpture, and for the names of the distinguished dead whose ashes lie buried within its walls. It lies upon the high and wooded bank of the Schuylkill, opposite the northern end of the

BRIDGE OVER NICETOWN LANE, IN LAUREL HILL CEMETERY.

SOUTH ENTRANCE TO LAUREL HILL CEMETERY, RIDGE AVENUE, PHILADELPHIA.

West Park. Just north of it is the busy suburban and industrial village of Falls of Schuylkill. It may be reached by the Ridge Avenue cars. Laurel Hill Cemetery is divided into three parts: South, Central, and North Laurel Hill, without reckoning the well-known West Laurel Hill, which is on the opposite side of the Schuylkill, towards the north-west. Laurel Hill, or "The Laurels," now North Laurel Hill, was originally the family estate of the Sims family, while Central Laurel Hill was "Fairy Hill," the country home of Mr. George Pepper; and South Laurel Hill was "Harleigh," once the seat of the Rawle family. Near the entrance to North Laurel Hill is an interesting sculptured group representing Old Mortality, his pony, and Sir Walter Scott, cut in brown-stone by the artist Thom. Across Ridge Avenue from Laurel Hill Cemetery is a group of smaller cemeteries, among them **Mount Vernon**, which contains some splendid examples of funereal sculpture, and **Mount Peace**, a large and beautiful burying-ground, owned by the Odd Fellows, and which may be regarded as an extension of the older Odd-Fellows' Cemetery, elsewhere noticed, which lies half a mile south-eastward from Mount Peace. The **Church of St. James the Less** (Episcopalian) stands in a small and very neatly-kept burial-ground, between Clearfield Street and Nicetown Lane, a short distance from the main entrance to North Laurel Hill. It is a small though strikingly beautiful church of stone, in the Early English style, with a remarkably fine interior. It was once celebrated all over the country as one of the choicest specimens of church architecture in the United States.

The ancient village of **Falls of Schuylkill**, also called Falls Village or The Falls, now in the Twenty-eighth ward, takes its name from certain rapids in the Schuylkill, now almost flooded out by the action of the dam at Fairmount. "The Falls" is almost entirely an industrial place. Great factories of stone furnish employment to a large proportion of the inhabitants, both male and female. The built-up section is on the north-east side of the river. The lines of the Philadelphia and Reading Railway run not far from the river, on either bank. The principal street lies near the river, the side-streets climbing the steep hill-sides at irregular intervals. The principal building of any architectural interest is the church of St. James the Less, previously noticed.

Of the manufactories at Falls of Schuylkill there are some which merit special notice, from their extent and importance. Of these we may particularly speak of the immense **Dobson Carpet-Mills**, the

NORTH ENTRANCE TO LAUREL HILL CEMETERY, RIDGE AVENUE, PHILADELPHIA.

largest in the United States, and employing several thousands of hands. Another mammoth concern is the **Powers & Weightman Chemical Manufactory**, already noticed as among the largest in the country. Just beyond Falls of Schuylkill, and below the mouth of the Wissahickon, we come to **School Lane**, one of the most beautiful suburban streets in the world.

A short distance above here, and just below the mouth of the Wissahickon, a new bridge crosses the Schuylkill at a very lofty elevation, affording charming views up and down this picturesque stream, with its winding, elevated, and well-wooded banks. Under it ply the Park steamboats, which make this section of the Park easily accessible. Starting from Fairmount, these boats stop successively at the Zoological Garden, at the rural island of Belmont Landing, at the cliff-bordered Rockland station, below the bluffs of Laurel Hill, and at other stations, ending their journey at the Wissahickon, where is a garden sacred to refreshment, both material and musical.

North-west from Falls of Schuylkill, across Wissahickon Creek, we come to **Manayunk**, in the Twenty-first Ward of Philadelphia, but

Manayunk. almost forming a city by itself. It is reached either by the Reading or the Pennsylvania Railroad, and by the Ridge Avenue cars. It is a busy manufacturing centre. Its steep streets, and the quaint uniformity of its older dwellings (generally of stone or brick, and plastered), and the ponderous solidity of its great stone mills, give it a peculiar and characteristic appearance. Above it, along the crest of the hills, stretches the fine old town of **Roxborough**, with many handsome residences.

Chief among the manufactures of Manayunk stands paper, it being the seat of the **Flat Rock Paper-Mills**, of Martin Nixon, and the mills of the **American Wood-Paper Company**, the two together forming the most extensive paper-works in the world. The most notable feature of Roxborough is its great reservoir, which is located at an elevation of four hundred and ninety feet, and has a capacity of one hundred and seventy-three million gallons.

Continuing up the Schuylkill, several places of minor interest are passed, among them the celebrated soapstone quarries, from which great quantities of this valuable material are obtained. Beautiful views present themselves as we follow the river northward, our journey in this direction ending at the busy industrial town of **Conshohocken**, twelve miles from the centre of the city, though just beyond its limits.

BELMONT LANDING.

XXIV.

UP THE WISSAHICKON.

Wissahickon Creek.
BEYOND Falls Village, a short distance brings us to the mouth of the **Wissahickon**, and as we turn our faces up its Drive the first object to attract our attention is the magnificent viaduct which carries the tracks of the Norristown branch of the Reading Railroad across the gorge. It is four hundred and ninety-two feet in length, twenty-eight feet wide, seventy feet high, and has five spans of sixty-five feet each. It is built of stone, and is a most substantial and, at the same time, graceful structure. Its noble

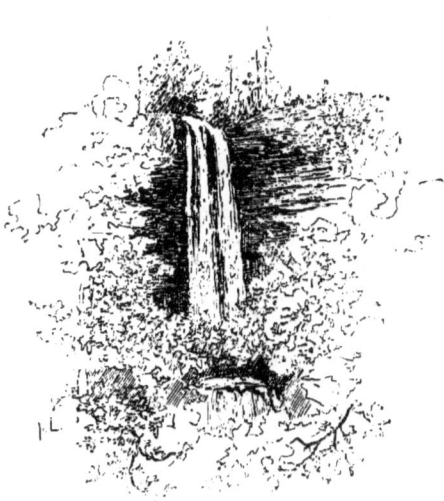

arches form a fitting portal to the beautiful and romantic valley which it spans, and which is one of the most remarkable regions ever included within the limits of a great city. Entering it from the heat and glare of a summer's day seems like penetrating Calypso's grotto, so dark and cool are its shaded precincts, with their mossy rocks, their trickling rills, and feathery ferns. In its lower part the Wissahickon has a placid, pool-like aspect, caused by the checking of its current by a dam thrown across near its mouth. This gives the stream a width and depth beyond what are natural to it, and makes this part of its course an admirable boating-ground for the picnic-parties and recreation-seekers who, from early morning till late in the evening, may, in the summer-time, be found disporting themselves upon its surface.

As we proceed, the drive, following the windings of the stream,

THE WISSAHICKON CREEK, FROM RIDGE AVENUE.

leads us beneath beetling crags and overhanging trees, the narrow valley-bottom occasionally broadening into a glade, and affording room for a house of entertainment, of which several are passed as we ascend the stream. Some of these are old-time structures, and their quaint picturesqueness makes them harmonious adjuncts to their romantic setting.

The Wissahickon in its upper course is a brawling, rapid stream, swirling around the boulders that intersperse its bed with an eddying

WISSAHICKON DRIVE.

sweep, which makes us think of trout; but those dainty exquisites of the finny tribe are not among its denizens. The Wissahickon was formerly much more prolific of fish than it is now. The erection of mills and the pollution of the water by their waste pretty much annihilated all but the very hardiest species. Now, however, the mills having been removed, an effort has been made to stock the stream with bass and other fish, and it is not improbable that, in the coming

VIEW OF THE WISSAHICKON.

years, its waters restored to their pristine purity, the Wissahickon may become as favorite a resort for the fisherman as it always has been for the poet, the artist, and the lover of nature.

As we advance along the beautiful drive on the western bank, our attention is arrested by a curious structure crossing the gorge high above our heads, different from anything we have heretofore seen. This is known as the Pipe Bridge. It is six hundred and eighty-four

VALLEY GREEN HOTEL.

feet long and one hundred feet above the creek. The pipes that supply Germantown with water form the chords of the bridge, the whole being bound together with wrought-iron. Near this is "Devil's Pool," a basin in Cresheim Creek, which rises in Montgomery County, and, flowing westwardly, here unites with the Wissahickon.

Valley Green Hotel is next reached, and affords a comfortable resting-place for man and beast. It is a quaint old wayside inn, a favorite house of call with the frequenters of the drive, and a tempting subject for artists, by whom it has been sketched time and again.

Half a mile beyond the Valley Green Hotel stands the first public fountain erected in Philadelphia. A lion's-head spout carries the water of a cold hill-side spring, niched in a granite arch, into a marble basin. Upon a slab of marble above the niche are the words "Pro bono publico," and beneath the basin is the legend "Esto perpetua." It was erected in 1854, and was the gift of Mr. Joseph Cook, a public-spirited citizen.

FROM DEVIL'S POOL TO INDIAN ROCK.

Near Valley Green is a stone bridge across the Wissahickon, from which a beautifully-shaded and well-kept road leads up the steep ascent, debouching upon the plateau above near the new Wissahickon Inn. To the left of this road, as it winds upward, may be caught a glimpse of the recently-erected palatial residence of Mr. H. H. Houston, one of the costliest and most magnificent private structures in or about Philadelphia. Through a mile and a half of rugged scenery above Valley Green we emerge into the smiling landscape of White Marsh Valley, and our delightful tour of the Wissahickon is at an end.

In addition to the carriage road, paths for pedestrians have been carried along the precipitate sides of this delightful valley, and these open up a succession of grand and striking views, which carry one on and on with ever new allurements, till miles are traversed almost unconsciously. This romantic ravine, with its graceful stream, forms a fitting complement to the broad levels, tasteful dells, rounded slopes, and liquid expanses of Fairmount Park, the combination being one of which Philadelphia may well be proud, since no other city in the world can point to a park possessed of such a diversity of natural attractions, so beautiful in themselves that art is hardly needed to enhance them.

A RESIDENCE NEAR LOGAN STATION.

XXV.

THE READING RAILROAD'S ROUTES.

LEAVING the Terminal Station at Twelfth and Market Streets, and proceeding over the elevated roadway to Callowhill Street, the **Philadelphia and Reading Railroad** branches into two divisions,—the **Main Line**, which leaves the city by way of Willow Street and Pennsylvania Avenue, and proceeds to Reading and points north; and the **New York Division**, which follows the line of Ninth Street, and, in addition to the Bound Brook Route, embraces the Germantown and Chestnut Hill, the Norristown, and the Bethlehem branches. At Bethlehem it continues over the Lehigh Valley tracks, now under Reading control. A third division, the **Philadelphia and Atlantic City**, has its stations at Chestnut Street and South Street Wharves.

Following the New York Division, we pass through a part of the city already described, reaching, some four miles out, the old-time village of **Nicetown**, principally notable at present from the **Midvale Steel-Works**, one of Philadelphia's great manufacturing establishments, here located. In the vicinity of Nicetown (at Nicetown Lane and Old York Road) is **Hunting Park**, the largest of the public pleasure-grounds of the northern section of the city, excepting Fairmount Park. It contains forty-three acres, and was formerly a race-course, but has been converted of recent years into a park.

The next station worthy of notice is **Wayne Junction**, where are extensive carpet- and cotton-mills. Here the trains for New York diverge from those for Germantown, and traverse a highly-cultivated section of great natural beauty, comprising many old estates, whose grand old mansions sit embowered in groves of trees which have witnessed the coming and going of generations of occupants, while among them are many handsome residences of a modern type, effectively situated.

Wayne Junction.

Some seven miles out, at **Fern Rock Station**, junction is made with the **Bethlehem Branch** (formerly the North Pennsylvania Railroad), on which, near **Tabor Station**, somewhat nearer the city, are the fine buildings erected by the **Jewish Hospital Association** (on Olney Road, near York Pike), embracing the **Hospital** proper, a handsome edifice of pointed stone, in a semi-

Jewish Hospital.

OGONTZ—WEST WING.

OGONTZ—EAST TOWER.

Moorish style of architecture, with accommodations for sixty-five patients; the **Mathilde Adler Loeb Dispensary** (free to all), founded in memory of the wife of Mr. August B. Loeb; and the **Home for Aged and Infirm Israelites**, which has a capacity for one hundred inmates. About two and a half miles beyond Fern Rock junction the station of **Ogontz** is reached, this name having been given to the old village formerly known as Shoemakertown.

A mile from Ogontz Village, crowning one of the wooded heights in the midst of the beautiful "Chelten Hills" region, five hundred feet above the Delaware River, stands the **Ogontz School Establishment for Young Ladies**, once a private residence of almost baronial grandeur, built at a cost of a million dollars or more by Mr. Jay Cooke, banker and railroad magnate, who, after a varied financial experience, a few years since leased the property to the present occupants—then the proprietors of the well-known Chestnut Street Seminary, Philadelphia—for educational purposes. Here, surrounded by wide acres of lawn, rises the main building of the establishment, a granite structure four and five stories in height, in dignity and spaciousness resembling an aristocratic country-seat of the Old World, and, in elegant appliances suited to its present use, with few or no equals among educational institutions.

Ogontz School.

Its spacious apartments embrace a drawing-room thirty by fifty feet in extent, a library thirty-five by forty, and a dining-room with a capacity for seating seventy-five guests. The main hall, seventeen feet wide and eighty feet long, terminates in a conservatory or winter-garden forty feet square. A massive stairway of solid walnut leads to some seventy-five upper rooms, the private apartments of teachers and pupils. In addition, there is an art building, an infirmary, a gymnasium, and various accessory structures.

The succeeding stations are **Chelten Hills** and **Jenkintown**, the latter of which (about eleven miles out) will end our journey in this direction. The village of Jenkintown, here situated, is the centre of a very attractive region, which has been taken advantage of as the site of numerous handsome country-seats.

Following the Germantown and Chestnut Hill Branch from Wayne Junction, the first station reached is **Fisher's**, through which passes the well-known Fisher's Lane. On this, eastward from the station, on Wingohocking Creek, are the quaint old **Wakefield Mills**, whose antiquity makes them worthy a visit. **Wister Station**, half a mile beyond, is on Wister Street, which is lined with handsome residences.

The succeeding station, which bears the euphonious name of **Wingohocking**, is notable as having in its vicinity a striking group of charitable institutions. These are situated on an eminence, sepa-

WAKEFIELD MILLS, GERMANTOWN.

rated from the station by a ravine. Here is the well-known **Germantown Hospital**, built for the benefit, primarily, of the large number of laborers employed in that vicinity, and entirely supported by private contributions. Near the Hospital is the **Jewish Foster Home and Orphan Asylum**, a favorite object of charity with benevolent Hebrews, where from seventy-five to one hundred children of either sex are supported and schooled. Here also is that estimable charity, the **Home for the Aged Poor of Both Sexes**, conducted by the "Little Sisters of the Poor," who dispense to the aged under their care (some three hundred) such contributions as they gather up in their periodical rounds among the charitably disposed. This Home, consisting of a connected group of spacious apartments, is one of over two hundred and fifty similar institutions maintained by this Order in various parts of the world.

The succeeding station, that known as **Chelten Avenue**, brings us to the centre of **Germantown**, the oldest, largest, and most attractive suburban settlement within the limits of Philadelphia, and possessing attractions which render it amply worthy a visit. The station named is situated near the intersection of Chelten Avenue and Main Street, the business centre of the place, while the remainder of the town is largely made up of the attractive residences of business people of Philadelphia. Germantown was the scene of a battle of the Revolution, of which it still possesses a famous relic in the old **Chew House**

Chew House.
(Main and Johnson Streets), a venerable stone mansion, which sheltered a portion of the British forces from an attack by the Americans, and enabled them in the end to defeat the latter. The old house still bears marks of the battle. Nearly opposite is the **Johnson House**, another venerable structure of much interest.

At **Walnut Lane Station**, a mile beyond, is the **Crematory and Columbarium** of the Philadelphia Cremation Society. The next point of interest on the line of the road is **Mount Airy**, a locality with many rural charms and the seat of some institutions of interest. Here, on Main Street, is the **Evangelical Lutheran Seminary**, which has an attendance of about seventy-five students and a library of twenty thousand volumes, especially rich in biblical and liturgical literature. A short distance south of the Seminary, on Main Street, is the **Lutheran Orphans' Home and Asylum for the Aged and Infirm**, its inmates numbering about seventy-five children and thirty-five aged people.

An institution of much greater general interest, recently established at Mount Airy, is the **Pennsylvania Institution for the Deaf and Dumb**, which was organized in 1821, and is the third oldest of its

kind in America. Opening with seven pupils, it has now an annual attendance of about four hundred and forty, and
since its establishment has afforded instruction to over
four thousand deaf children. In addition to manual and
oral speech and intellectual instruction, the pupils are
given industrial training in such branches as wood-working, shoe-
making, printing, sewing, dress-making, etc. This institution long occupied extensive premises at Broad and Pine Streets, but in 1892 was
removed to its suburban quarters. The new buildings occupy a tract
of seventy acres, and are delightfully situated, commodious, well

Deaf and Dumb Institution.

THE MERMAID INN.

lighted, and admirably adapted to their purpose. They have accommodation for five hundred and fifty inmates. The Institution is
claimed by its managers to be now the largest, most convenient, and
most complete school for the deaf in the world.

Nearly a half-mile from Mount Airy Station is **Mermaid Station**,
near which, at the intersection of Main Street and Mermaid Lane, is
an old-time hostelry known as the **Mermaid Inn**, which has escaped
the iconoclastic hand of the modern reconstructionist, and stands in
all its pristine picturesqueness a quaint old memorial of bygone days.
Near the inn is another object almost as interesting as the old inn

itself. This is a log house which, though now rapidly falling to decay, has stood since 1743, when it was built by Christopher Seakle, a German cooper, who for years lived and plied his trade there. The road reaches its terminus at **Chestnut Hill**, about eleven miles from the Market Street Station, the highest tract of land, and one of the most attractive spots, within the limits of Philadelphia.

The allied Norristown Branch of the Reading's system presents few points of interest not already described. Diverging from the Germantown Branch at Sixteenth Street, it follows the Schuylkill, with stations at Falls of Schuylkill, School Lane, Wissahickon, Manayunk, and various other river-side places of more or less attraction, taking Conshohocken in its route, and ending at the handsome city of Norristown, the county-seat of Montgomery County, about seventeen miles out.

The Main Line Division, which crosses the river at Columbia Bridge, in the Park limits, and follows the west side of the Schuylkill, presents no points of special interest within the city limits. At Pencoyd Station, opposite Manayunk and near West Laurel Hill Cemetery, are the extensive **Pencoyd Iron-Works**, one of the largest in the vicinity of the city. Passing through West Conshohocken and Bridgeport (opposite Norristown), it reaches, about twenty-four miles out, the interesting historical locality of **Valley Forge**, the celebrated site of the encampment of Washington's army during the terrible winter of 1777–78.

XXVI.

THE PENNSYLVANIA RAILROAD'S ROUTES.

FROM the central station at Broad and Market Streets the Pennsylvania Railroad lines extend through a wide section of country, its routes including the **Main Line**, running westward to Pittsburgh, with several important branches; the **Philadelphia, Wilmington and Baltimore Road**, going southward; the **Media and West Chester Road**, running south-westward; the **New York Division**, with its **Germantown and Chestnut Hill Branch**; and the **Schuylkill Valley Division**, leading northward.

Following the **Main Line** outwards, the first place of interest to be noted is at **Overbrook Station**, five and a half miles from Broad Street, near which is located the Roman Catholic **Theological Seminary of St. Charles Borromeo**. Some two miles farther out is **Elm Station**, a half-mile north of which is the **Belmont Driving Park**, elsewhere noticed. Near it are schools of the **Franciscan Sisters**. Fine country-seats abound in this vicinity. The next station of importance is **Ardmore**, beyond which is the handsome borough of **Haverford College**, which

Haverford College. owes its title to the flourishing institution of the same name, the leading high-class college in this country conducted by the Orthodox Friends. It was founded as a school in 1830, and in 1856 invested with the full rank of a college. The institution is beautifully situated, and has very commodious buildings, which are surrounded by a campus of sixty acres of well-kept lawns and grounds. Near Haverford Station are the new **Merion Cricket Club Grounds**, where is a commodious club-house, and grounds which are claimed to be the finest of their kind in the world.

One mile from Haverford College, and ten and two-tenths miles from Broad Street Station, is the village of **Bryn Mawr** (Welsh for "Great Ridge"), consisting largely of elegant country-seats, notable among which is the villa of George W. Childs, Esq., said to be one of the finest places in the vicinity of Philadelphia. Especially to be mentioned as among the attractions of the village is **Bryn Mawr**

Bryn Mawr College. **College**, for the advanced education of women, which was endowed by the late Dr. Joseph W. Taylor, of Burlington, New Jersey, and opened for instruction in 1885.

Several elegant stone structures, containing class-rooms and rooms for students, constitute the principal buildings of the institution, besides which there is a large and complete gymnasium for the use of students, residences for the professors, etc. The grounds occupy forty acres, and the buildings are beautifully located about a half-mile from the railroad station. Bryn Mawr College is a school of the first rank. A half-mile from Bryn Mawr is **Rosemont Station**, three-fourths of a mile from which, on the Lancaster Pike, is the **Hospital of the Good Shepherd**, a Protestant Episcopal institution, where are received for treatment invalid children of from two to twelve years of age, without regard to creed or country. Eleven and nine-tenths miles from Broad Street, at the station of **Villa Nova**, is **Villa Nova College and Monastery**, a Roman Catholic institution, with extensive grounds and commodious buildings, conducted by the Hermit Fathers of the Order of St. Augustine. A farm of two hundred and thirty acres is attached to the Monastery, and worked by the lay brothers. Thirteen miles from Broad Street is the village of **Radnor**, which, in common with other places in that section, has many beautiful country-seats in its environs. About a mile and a half from Radnor is the beautiful borough of **Wayne**, one of the most attractive and rapidly-improving *new* places within the environs of Philadelphia. Fine residences, built with due regard to architectural beauty, are rapidly springing up in all sections of the community, and a strikingly attractive Protestant Episcopal church, of Gothic architecture, has recently been built, which is said to be the handsomest suburban church in the State. There are here two excellent summer hotels, the **Louella** and the **Bellevue**. In the vicinity is the summer home of the Lincoln Institution, already noticed. The next station of interest is **Devon**, its principal attraction being its fine summer hotel, **Devon Inn**, a fashionable resort much patronized in the summer. Fine country-seats abound in this vicinity, and near here are two recently established charitable institutions: the **Home for Convalescents**, endowed by Lady Kortright, formerly a Philadelphian, and the **Eliza Cathcart Home for Incurables**, endowed by the late William S. Stroud (of the Baldwin Locomotive-Works). These institutions are both under the management of the Presbyterian Hospital, and possess large and handsome buildings, excellently adapted to their purpose. Two and a half miles south of Devon is an edifice of ante-Revolutionary fame, old **St. David's Church** (Protestant Episcopal). This quaint old building, the veteran of the district, and nearly the oldest church in the State, stands in a strikingly rural situation, and is worth a visit as a relic of the past.

Schuylkill Valley R. R. The route of the Schuylkill Valley Division of the Pennsylvania Railroad System extends generally northward from Broad Street Station to outlying districts partly through territory untraversed by other railroads, and partly through towns and villages whose railroad facilities are enhanced by competing lines. For a short distance this route may be said to lie within the environs of Philadelphia.

Park Station. On leaving the Broad Street Station, for the first four miles the trains follow the tracks of the Main Line of the Pennsylvania Railroad until Fifty-second Street Station is reached, when, diverging to the right, they take the track of the Schuylkill Valley Route proper, for Manayunk, Norristown, and intermediate places. About a half-mile from Fifty-second Street (and the first stopping place beyond) is **Park Station**, near which is that section of Fairmount Park known as George's Hill, one of the most attractive points in the Park, and from the summit of which is obtained a fine view in the direction of the city. Just beyond Park Station, on the right of the railroad, is the **Children's Convalescent Hospital**, a branch of the Children's Hospital at Twenty-second and Walnut Streets (see INDEX). This institution occupies a neat and unpretentious stone building, open only in the summer and autumn months. It was first occupied in June, 1889. Here the convalescent children of the main hospital are taken for a few weeks of country air,—the children all receiving the same kind attention, whether their parents are able to pay for it or not.

Christ Church Hospital. At no great distance from the Convalescent Hospital stands the handsome **Christ Church Hospital**,—in reality a home for ladies, whether widows or spinsters,—connected with the Protestant Episcopal Church. This most excellent charity was founded in 1772 by Dr. John Kearsley, and further endowed, in 1804, by Joseph Dobbins, of South Carolina. The towers of the main building, "bosomed high in tufted trees," may be seen near the railway, and on the right hand as the train moves from Philadelphia. The present fine building was finished and opened in 1857. Just beyond the Christ Church Hospital stands the **Hayes Mechanics' Home**, founded in 1858 by George Hayes, for the reception of disabled or aged and infirm American Mechanics of good character. The Home is entirely non-sectarian, and any person who is a fit subject for its charity is admitted on the payment, by his friends or others, of a moderate fee. Connected with this Home is a substantial building for mechanical work, in which such of the inmates as are able to do any work can find such employment as may help them to pass a portion of their time.

As the train nears the pretty suburban village of Bala (five and seven-tenths miles out), a passing glimpse may be had of the beautiful **Orphanage of the Methodist Episcopal Church,**—a noble

Methodist Episcopal Orphanage.

edifice of stone,—standing somewhat less than half a mile from the railway track. The very praiseworthy charity does great credit to the heads and hearts of those who conceived it. The present building was first occupied in September, 1889, and receives both boys and girls. At the proper age the boys are sent away to suitable places in the country, chiefly on farms. The village of **Bala** is one of the pleasantest and neatest of Philadelphia's newer suburbs. Its name, like those of many

Bala Village.

other places in the vicinity, is of Welsh origin, and forms one of the many traces of the large Welsh element among the early Quaker colonists. The village is well built, many of the residences being stone-built cottages of quaint architectural design. St. Asaph's Church (Protestant Episcopal), a costly and very beautiful structure, is one of the architectural features of the village. The railroad station at Bala stands in Montgomery County, but is very near the line of Philadelphia.

Passing **Cynwyd Station** (a half-mile from Bala), the germ of what promises to become, on account of its high and healthy situation, a favorite residence locality for city business-men, the route of the railroad leads to the station of **West Laurel Hill** (seven miles from Broad Street), a cemetery covering one hundred and ten acres of ground, and one of the best-kept and most beautiful of the "cities of the dead" which are to be seen near the outskirts of the city.

The route of the **New York Division** follows the tracks of the Main Line past **Powelton Avenue** (the general West-Philadelphia

New York Division.

station), the **Zoological Garden** being its first separate station. Here it crosses the Schuylkill on a lofty iron bridge, adjoining the Girard Avenue Bridge, whence for miles it runs in a straight line past several city stations, the most important being that of **Germantown Junction.** Thence it passes through a section which we have already traversed, including Frankford, Bridesburg, Tacony, and other stations, to Trenton and beyond. The places of interest on this route have been sufficiently described.

The **Germantown and Chestnut Hill Branch** diverges from the New York Division at Germantown Junction, pursuing a route west of that of the Reading line to these points, and distant from it from half a mile to a mile. About two miles from the junction is Cricket Station, near the grounds of the **Germantown Cricket Club**, which are also near Nicetown Station, on the Reading Railroad.

Germantown Cricket Club. These grounds have been the scene of several notable international games between Philadelphia cricketers and the picked clubs of England and Ireland.

Queen Lane Station, in the vicinity of which are many fine country-seats, is succeeded by **Chelten Avenue Station**, around which spreads the most attractive residence section of Germantown. Near Chelten Station, and parallel with the Avenue, passes **School Lane**, already spoken of, which extends from Main Street to near the Schuylkill River, a distance of perhaps two miles, and is lined through nearly its entire length with fine residences, some of them unsurpassed in attractiveness by any within the environs of Philadelphia. On this Lane, near Main Street, is the venerable Germantown Academy, erected in 1760-61, "for the purpose of an English and High Dutch or German School," one of the oldest institutions of the kind in the city.

The route continues through various stations, each the centre of an attractive residence section, but whose places of particular interest we have noticed in connection with the parallel Reading Railroad. Beyond Mount Airy, and eleven miles from Broad Street Station, is the station of **Wissahickon Heights**, near which is the well-known **Wissahickon Inn**, a fashionable summer hotel, much patronized by the *élite* of Philadelphia, several hundreds of whom find accommodations here during "the season." A mile farther on is Chestnut Hill, the terminal station of the road.

Chestnut Hill. Chestnut Hill has been for years to Philadelphia a synonyme for whatever is attractive in a suburban community. Elegant residences cover its high-lying grounds and slopes, from which beautiful views of valleys and heights beyond meet the eye in every direction. Among the institutions here is the **Home for Consumptives**, of the Protestant Episcopal City Mission (already mentioned), and the **Bethesda Children's Christian Home**, a most meritorious charity, which now occupies four buildings, and cares for some two hundred little inmates of either sex.

The two southerly routes of the Pennsylvania Railroad separate near South Street Station, the Wilmington Branch passing near several charitable institutions already mentioned (the Home for Incurables, the Presbyterian Home for Women, and the Presbyterian Orphanage), beyond which, at Mount Moriah Station, is the well-known **Mount Moriah Cemetery**, much visited during the summer. The road passes on through a series of attractive towns and villages, occupied principally by business people of Philadelphia, the most attractive of which is **Ridley Park**, ten and a half miles out, and the seat of numerous handsome residences. Thirteen and a half miles from Broad Street is the thriving city of **Chester**, of whose river-side manufactories we have already spoken.

P. W. & B. Railroad.

Chester. Chester is the oldest place in the State of Pennsylvania, having been settled in 1643 by the Swedes, who called it Upland. It was long a quiet old town, but has been growing rapidly of recent years, and has now a population of over twenty thousand. Its growth is due to its manufacturing importance, its great ship-yard, print-works, steel-works, machine-shops, cotton-mills, etc., making it a stirring and prosperous place. There are in its vicinity two educational institutions of importance,—the **Crozer Theological Seminary**, a Baptist institution of high standing, and the **Pennsylvania Military College**, an educational establishment of sufficient importance to merit an extended description. This College was incorporated in 1862 as the Pennsylvania Military Academy, the title of College being adopted in 1892. It stands on a commanding eminence in the north-west section of the city, and comprises a Main Building, four stories high, two hundred and seventeen feet long and fifty feet wide, and accessory buildings, including a Drill-Hall, a Riding-Hall, a Gymnasium, and a Laboratory, all of ample dimensions. The grounds are large, a portion of them of nine acres in area being laid out as a parade-ground. There are four collegiate courses of instruction, the Civil Engineering, the Chemical, the Architectural, and the Academic, each of four years' duration. The Military instruction comprises a theoretical course in infantry and artillery tactics and the elements of military science, and a practical course in infantry and artillery drill and other military exercises and duties, with an optional cavalry drill. In these exercises all students must take part. The institution is supplied with arms and artillery by the United States Ordnance Department.

The **West Chester Branch** of the Pennsylvania Railroad is similarly

PENNSYLVANIA MILITARY COLLEGE.—OFF FOR A PRACTICE MARCH.

PENNSYLVANIA MILITARY COLLEGE.—BATTERY DRILL.

lined with growing residence-towns for the overflow of the population of Philadelphia. Its most notable station, something over eleven miles from Broad Street Station, is Swarthmore the seat of Swarthmore College, the principal educational establishment in the United States of the Hicksite branch of the Society of Friends. The principal college buildings are massive structures of stone. Other buildings are the Science Hall, the Astronomical Observatory, and houses for the families of professors, one of whom occupies the historical West House, the birthplace of the celebrated American painter, Benjamin West. Two hundred and forty acres of land are occupied, half of which are devoted to lawns and pleasure-grounds. Students of either sex are admitted. About a mile from Swarthmore is Wallingford Station, surrounded by country-seats of wealthy Philadelphians, some of whom, on their highly-cultivated farms, make a specialty of breeding fancy stock and blooded horses.

To Media and West Chester.

Swarthmore College.

Fourteen miles from Broad Street Station is the pretty borough of Media, the county-seat of Delaware County, situated on elevated ground and with highly-attractive surroundings. It has the distinction that no liquor has ever been allowed to be sold as a beverage within its limits. One mile beyond Media is Elwyn Station, the seat of the Delaware County Fair Grounds and of the Pennsylvania Training-School for Feeble-Minded Children, a most deserving charity, which has given a home to eight hundred and fifty children of this helpless class. It is divided into four departments,—the Asylum, Nursery, School, and Industrial,—in accordance with the condition of its occupants, and is doing an excellent work.

Media Borough.

School for Feeble-Minded Children.

At Williamson Station, nearly a mile beyond Elwyn, and about sixteen miles from the city, may be seen one of those noble charitable institutions which give such honor to Philadelphia, the Williamson Free School of Mechanical Trades. This institution is richly endowed, it having been established under a bequest by the late I. V. Williamson of $2,250,000, all of which is intact, the buildings having been erected from the income of this bequest. These buildings include a large administration edifice, an engine-house (with electric-light plant), workshops, superintendent's and teachers' houses, and a number of cottages, the dwelling-places of the inmates. The family-plan has been adopted, each cottage being under the control of a matron, the wife of one of

Williamson Mechanical School.

the teachers where available. The institution contains at present about one hundred and twenty boys, but it is proposed to have in all about five hundred. Tuition, board, clothing, etc., are entirely free, and the students are given a good English education, are instructed in drawing and designing, and are thoroughly taught some trade,— their own choice being consulted. The trades at present taught are house-building, machine and other iron work, pattern-making, carpentry, plumbing, and electrical engineering. Farming will also probably be taught, the grounds containing about two hundred acres of land. As to the character of the instruction, it may be stated that the class of bricklayers and carpenters build a complete house, even to making its architectural plans and working drawings. The building is then taken down, to be rebuilt by the next class. This institution cannot fail to be of the highest usefulness. It is in the line of the most advanced modern ideas of education, but differs from manual training-schools in that it teaches complete trades. It is well worthy a visit from all who are interested in educational progress.

At **Glen Mills Station**, about twenty miles from Broad Street, may be seen the new plant of the **House of Refuge**, which has recently been removed to this locality. This institution was incorporated in 1826 as a private charity for the reclamation of idle and depraved children, but has been generously supported by public aid. For many years it was situated on Poplar Street, between Twenty-second and Twenty-fourth Streets, but in 1892 was removed to the locality here named, where much more ample accommodations had been prepared for the five hundred and twenty-five boys then under its care. The purpose of this removal was the praiseworthy one of doing away with the prison-like character of the institution, and detaining the inmates by interest rather than by force. This system, which has been successfully tried in several States, is known as the cottage system, the boys being distributed among a number of cottages, as in the Williamson School, just described, and thus divided into family groups, each under the care of what may be called a father and mother, while no walls enclose the buildings, and there are no signs of detention visible. The institution is complete in itself, having its own railroad service, electric-light plant, chapel, schools, workshops, etc. The trades taught are shoe-making, cane-chair-making, brush-making, tailoring, printing, carpentering, masonry, blacksmithery, etc., while agriculture is diligently prosecuted, there being three hundred and eighty-five acres within the area enclosed. There is great reason to believe that this new system will work much better than the old one of strict detention within city limits.

Some three and a half miles beyond Glen Mills is the station of **Westtown**, near which is the celebrated **Westtown School**, a Friends' boarding-school which has long been notable in this vicinity. The road reaches its terminus at **West Chester**, twenty-seven miles from the city, and an attractive old town which is well worth a visit.

The **Baltimore and Ohio Railroad**, whose station is at Twenty-fourth and Chestnut Streets, runs southward parallel and in close proximity to the Philadelphia, Wilmington and Baltimore Railroad, their stations being frequently close together. The places of interest on the two roads are the same, and no further description of them is necessary.

XXVIII.

TO CAMDEN AND BEYOND.

Ferry Lines to Camden. SEVERAL lines of Ferries, operated for the most part as terminals to railroads that converge at Camden, connect that city with Philadelphia, the principal lines, commencing on the north, being the **Shackamaxon Ferry**, which plies between Shackamaxon Street, Kensington, and Vine Street, Camden (where is located the Camden and Atlantic City Railroad Station); the **Vine Street Ferry**, running from Vine Street, Philadelphia, to Vine Street, Camden; the **Market Street and Federal Street Ferries**, running from Market Street, Philadelphia, respectively, to Market Street and Federal Street, Camden (the latter connecting with the New Jersey branches of the Pennsylvania Railroad); the **Reading Railroad Company's Ferries**, from their stations near Chestnut Street and South Street wharves, to Kaighn's Point, Camden, where connection is made with the **Philadelphia and Atlantic City Division** of the Reading Railroad; and the **Gloucester Ferries**, from Arch Street and South Street wharves to **Gloucester**, New Jersey, about three miles distant.

Though still, to a considerable extent, a city of residences for parties doing business in Philadelphia, the increasing manufactures of Camden are rapidly changing its character to that of an extensive industrial city, its favorable location, bounded on the one side by the navigable Delaware and on the others by practically limitless, available territory for building-sites, rendering the place peculiarly well adapted to manufacturing purposes.

Industries of Camden. Among its numerous industrial establishments are extensive nickel smelting-works, chemical works, ship-building yards, iron-works, machine-shops, dye-works, and manufactures of woollen, glass, oil-cloths, soaps, steel pens, etc. Its public institutions comprise a fine new Court-House, a City Hall, a Hospital (called the **Cooper Hospital**, from the name of its founder),

Public Institutions. Children's Homes, for both white and colored children (the latter under the care of members of the Society of Friends), numerous Churches, and three National Banks.

Horse-railroads traverse the streets of the city, and from the ferry-landings steam railroad lines extend into the country in several directions, the most important being the sea-shore routes, whose patrons to the various points on the New Jersey Coast are numbered, in the season, by the tens of thousands.

These railroad routes include the **West Jersey**, running to **Cape May**, with branches to **Atlantic City** and various other sea-side resorts, and to a number of South Jersey towns; the **Camden and Atlantic**, to Atlantic City; the Pennsylvania Railroad route *via* **Mount Holly** to **Barnegat, Seaside Park, Manasquan, Ocean Grove, Asbury Park, Long Branch**, etc.; the **Camden and Amboy**, with branches to **Long Branch**, etc.; and the Reading Railroad routes to Atlantic City and various inland towns. Of the points of interest reached by these lines, those which lie along the river have already been mentioned. Of the inland towns may be named the thriving village of **Palmyra**; the borough of **Merchantville**, principally inhabited by Philadelphians, near which is the **Merchantville Race-Course**; the old-time borough of **Moorestown**, eleven miles inland, one of the most attractive towns of that section; and the thriving town of **Mount Holly**, some twenty miles from Philadelphia, and the seat of large carpet-mills and other manufactories. The borough of **Haddonfield**, on the Camden and Atlantic Railroad, about seven miles from the city, contains many attractive residences, chiefly the homes of Philadelphians; and the same may be said of the city of **Woodbury**, a thriving manufacturing and residence place, on the West Jersey route, a little over eight miles away. Several miles southward is **Glassboro'**, notable for its large glass-works, some of which have been in operation for more than a century; half-way to the ocean is **Hammonton**, a busy centre of the fruit-growing industry; while nearer the sea is the city of **Egg Harbor**, largely a German settlement, where grapes are grown in profusion, and whose native wines have a wide celebrity. Another celebrated grape-growing settlement is **Vineland**, on the Cape May route; beyond which is the active town of **Millville**. Branches of the road from Glassboro' lead to the cities of **Salem** and **Bridgeton**.

But, so far as Philadelphians are concerned, the two places of most interest to be reached *via* Camden are the notable sea-side resorts,

Cape May | **Cape May** and **Atlantic City**, places distinctively affiliated with the Quaker City. The first named of these, at the extreme southern end of the State, has been a fashionable resort for generations, its magnificent beach having few equals

WASHINGTON MONUMENT.

for surf-bathing in the world. Near by is **Cape May Point**, a favorite summer resort of President Harrison. Of late years Cape May has settled into a quiet and dignified respectability, its former bustling activity being largely drafted off by its younger rival, **Atlantic City**, whose nearness to Philadelphia (about fifty-five miles by the shortest route), and its abundant and rapid railroad service, have made it the favorite of all those to whom time and cost are of importance. Atlantic City is an extensive cluster of hotels, boarding cottages, and private cottages, with accommodations for very many thousands of guests during the season. Its institutions directly associated with Philadelphia are the **Children's Sea-shore House**, founded in 1872, and the first of its kind in the United States, with accommodations for about one hundred and twenty-five invalid children and thirty mothers, and the **Sea-side House for Invalid Women**, in which about eight hundred women are annually received at a very low price for board, nursing, and medical attendance. Both of these are highly useful institutions. There are several other South Jersey sea-shore places reached by rail from Philadelphia, including **Longport, Ocean City, Sea Isle City, Avalon, Anglesea, Holly Beach**, and others, each with its own attractions for those who wish to enjoy the pleasures of a quiet sea-side residence and to whom the bustle and dissipation of a fashionable resort are a vexation to the spirit. And so, with this brief glance at what may be called the sea-side suburbs of Philadelphia, whither the weary denizens of the city streets betake themselves in multitudes during the summer heats to breathe the cool and health-giving airs of old ocean, and which are rapidly becoming a resort for invalids during the cooler months, we take our leave of the good City of Brotherly Love, after a series of walks through its precincts that have revealed to us a host of admirable institutions, and a number of edifices and industries which have no peers in this country, if in the world.

Before bidding Philadelphia a final farewell, however, some mention is desirable of the **Washington Monument**, the most striking work of art in the city. This, a grand equestrian statue, with a lofty and richly-ornamented stone base, the work of Professor Siemering, of Berlin, is the outcome of subscriptions which were begun by the Society of the Cincinnati in 1819, the amount available being now about a quarter million of dollars. The monument, of which an illustration is given on the preceding page, will soon be erected in a suitable location.

INDEX.

A.

Academy of Fine Arts, 24.
Academy of Music, 102.
Academy of Music (Illustration), 101.
Academy of Natural Sciences, 94.
Academy of the Sacred Heart, 94.
Academy of the Sisters of Notre Dame, 83.
Acorn Club, 107.
Aimwell School for Female Children, 51.
Aldine Hotel, 85.
Aldine Hotel (Illustration), 86.
Almshouse, Blockley, 167.
American Catholic Historical Society, 73.
American Life Insurance Company, 69.
American Philosophical Society, 58.
American Steamship Line, 149.
American Sunday-School Union, 35.
American Tract Society, 35.
American Trust Company, 123.
American Wood-Paper Company, 199.
Andalusia, Village of, 162.
Angora, District of, 172.
Apartment Houses, 52.
Appraiser's Building (U. S.), 143.
Apprentices' Library, 80.
Arch Street Meeting (Friends'), 81.
Ardmore, Village of, 216.
Armory of First Regiment, 123.
Armory of First Regiment (Illustr'n), 124.
Armory of First Troop City Cavalry, 88.
Armory of Second Regiment, 79, 126.
Armory of State Fencibles, 30.
Armory of Third Regiment, 110.
Art Club of Philadelphia, 102.
Art Club of Philadelphia (Illustration), 103.
Association Hall, 35.
Asylum of the Magdalen Society, 98.
Asylum of the Rosine Association, 100.
Athenæum Library and Reading-Room, 73.
Athletic Club of the Schuylkill Navy, 97.
Athletic Club of the Schuylkill Navy (Illustration), 96.
Atlantic City, 228.

B.

Bala, Village of, 219.
Baldwin Locomotive Works, 119.
Baldwin Locomotive Works (Illustr'n), 120.
Baltimore and Ohio R. R. Station, 88, 226.
Baltimore and Ohio Railroad Station (Illustration), 89.
Bank of North America, 69.
Baptist Board of Publication, 35.
Baptist Historical Society, 35.
Baptist Home for Women, 131.
Baptist Home for Women (Illustr'n), 132.
Baptist Orphanage, 172.
Bartram's Garden, 117.
Base-Ball Park, Philadelphia, 128.
Baugh & Sons' Chemical Works, 148.
Bear Pits, Zoological Garden (Illustration), 177.
Bedford Street Mission, 150.
Belmont Driving Park, 194, 216.
Belmont Landing (Illustration), 200.
Belmont Mansion, 193.
Belmont Reservoir, 193.
Belmont Water-Works, 193.
Bement, Miles & Co. Machine-Works, 187.
Beneficial Saving-Fund Society, 39.

Bergner & Engel's Brewery, 185.
Bethany Presbyterian Church, 117.
Bethesda Children's Christian Home, 220.
Betz (John F.) & Son's Brewery, 141.
Betz Building, 31.
Beverly, City of, 162.
Biddle Law Library, 33.
Blind Asylum, 98.
Blind Men's Working Home, 173.
Blind Women's Industrial Home, 174.
Blockley Almshouse, 167.
Board of Trade, Philadelphia, 63.
Bordentown, Borough of, 163.
Boston Steamship Line, 146.
Boulevard, 100.
Bourse, Philadelphia, 62.
Boys' High School, 121.
Bridesburg District and Arsenal, 155.
Bridge over Nicetown Lane (Illus.), 195.
Bridgeton, City of, 228.
Bristol, Borough of, 163.
Broad Street Station (P. R. R.), 31.
Broad Street Station, P. R. R. (Illus.), 32.
Bromley (John) & Son's Mills, 154.
Brown Brothers & Company's Building, 66.
Browning Society, 39.
Bryn Mawr, Village of, 216.
Bryn Mawr College, 216.
Bullitt Building, 70.
Bullitt Building (Illustration), 71.
Burd Orphan Asylum, 175.
Burlington, City of, 163.
Bush Hill Iron-Works, 119.
Bustleton, District of, 158.

C.

Cable Road, Market Street (Illustr'n), 54.
Caledonian Carpet Mills, 182.
Caledonian Club, 122.
Camden, City of, 227.
Camden and Atlantic Railroad, 139, 228.
Camden National Bank, 143.

Cape May City, 228.
Cape May Point, 230.
Carpenters' Hall, 70.
Carpenters' Hall (Illustration), 72.
Cathedral Cemetery, 175.
Cathedral, Roman Catholic, 93.
Cathedral, Roman Catholic (Illustr'n), 92.
Catholic High School, 27.
Catholic High School (Illustration), 29.
Catholic Historical Society, 73.
Catholic Home for Destitute Children, 94.
Catholic Total Abstinence Fountain, 192.
Catholic Total Abstinence Fountain (Illustration), 193.
Cedar Hill Cemetery, 157.
Central High School, 121.
Central News Company, 73.
Central Saving-Fund, 39.
Central Sick-Diet Kitchen, 149.
Chamouni Lake and Concourse, 194.
Chelton Avenue, 220.
Chelton Hills, 211.
Chester, City of, 161, 221.
Chestnut Hill District, 215, 220.
Chestnut Street National Bank, 60.
Chew House, 213.
Children's Convalescent Hospital, 218.
Children's Homœopathic Hospital, 125.
Children's Hospital of Philadelphia, 88.
Children's Sanitarium, 161.
Children's Seashore House, 230.
Christ Church, 141.
Christ Church (Illustration), 142.
Christ Church Hospital, 218.
Christ Memorial Church, 170.
Church Home for Children, 172.
Church Home for Seamen, 150.
Church of St. James the Greater, 170.
Church of St. James the Less, 197.
Church of the Gesù, 135.
Church of the Holy Trinity (P. E.), 83.
Church of the Holy Trinity (R. C.), 73.
Church of the Messiah, 126.

City Hall, 19.
City Hall (Illustration), 21, 22.
City Hall (Old), 56.
City Institute, Philadelphia, 85.
City Mission (Protestant Episcopal), 149.
City Trust and Safe Deposit Company, 48.
Clover Club, 107.
Clyde Steamship Lines, 139.
College of Pharmacy, Philadelphia, 51.
College of Pharmacy (Illustration), 50.
College of Physicians, Philadelphia, 106.
Columbia Avenue Saving-Fund, 126.
Columbia Club, 125.
Commercial Exchange, 143.
Commercial Union Assurance Company, 69.
Congress Hall (Old), 57.
Conshohocken, Town of, 199.
Contemporary Club, 107.
Cooper Hospital, 227.
Corn Exchange National Bank, 143.
Country Week, Children's, 39.
County Prison, 157.
Cramp's Ship-Yard, 153.
Crematory and Columbarium, 213.
Cricket Club, Germantown, 220.
Cricket Club, Merion, 216.
Crozer's Theological Seminary, 221.
Custom House (United States), 65.
Custom House, U. S. (Illustration), 66.

D.

Deaf and Dumb Institution, 213.
Delanco, Town of, 162.
Delaware Mutual Insurance Company, 69.
Devil's Pool to Indian Rock (Illus.), 206.
Devon Inn, 217.
Disston Saw-Works, 157.
Dobson's Carpet-Mills, 197.
Dolan's Keystone Knitting-Mills, 154.
Dreer's (Henry A.) Seed Farm, 162.
Drexel Building, 63.
Drexel Building (Illustration), 64.

Drexel (Mary J.) Home, 135.
Drexel (Mary J.) Home (Illustr'n), 136.
Drexel Institute, 167.
Drexel Institute (Illustration), 168.
Dupont Powder-Works, 161.
Dying Lioness (Illustration), 177.

E.

Earle's Picture Galleries, 53.
Eastern Penitentiary, 138.
East Park Reservoir, 185.
Edgewater, Village of, 162.
Egg Harbor City, 228.
Educational Home for Indian Boys, 171.
Edwin Forrest Home, 158.
Edwin Forrest Home (Illustration), 159.
Eliza Cathcart Home for Incurables, 217.
Episcopal Academy, 104.
Episcopal Divinity School, 171.
Episcopal Hospital, 152.
Erben, Search & Co.'s Zephyr-Works, 182.
Express Companies, 18.

F.

Fair-Hill Square, 153.
Fairmount Machine-Works, 182.
Fairmount Park Art Association, 184.
Fairmount Water-Works, 179.
Falls of Schuylkill Village, 197.
Farmers' Market, 43.
Farmers' and Mechanics' Nat'l Bank, 65.
Female Society for the Relief and Employment of the Poor, 62.
Ferries to Camden, etc., 227.
Fidelity Insurance Company, 66.
Fire Association Building, 69.
First National Bank, 66.
First Presbyterian Church, 75.
First Unitarian Church, 85.
Fish and Oyster Business (Illustr'n), 144.
Fish and Produce Business, (Illus.), 143.

Fitler (E. H.) & Co.'s Cordage Works, 156.
Fort Mifflin, 161.
Foster Home, 138.
Fourth National Bank, 71.
Franciscan Sisters, Schools of, 216.
Frankford, District of, 156.
Frankford Arsenal, 156.
Franklin Institute, 60.
Franklin's Grave, 81.
Franklin's Grave (Illustration), 81.
Franklin Reformatory Home for Inebriates, 48.
Franklin Square, 78.
Friends' Arch Street Meeting, 81.
Friends' Asylum for the Insane, 156.
Friends' Central School, 30.
Friends' Library, 30.
Friends' Meeting (Hicksite), 30.
Friends' Orange Street Meeting, 75.
Friends' Select School, 30.
Fruit Business (Illustration), 145.

G.

George's Hill, 192.
German Hospital, 135.
German Society of Pennsylvania, 79.
German Society (Illustration), 80.
Germantown, Suburb of, 213, 220.
Germantown Academy, 220.
Germantown Cricket Club, 220.
Germantown Hospital, 212.
Girard College, 133.
Girard College (Illustration), 134.
Girard Life and Trust Company, 33.
Girard National Bank, 69.
Girard Point Elevator, 113.
Girard Point Storage Company, 113, 148.
Girls' Normal Schools, 122.
Glassboro', Borough of, 228.
Gloucester, City of, 146, 160.
Grace Baptist Church, 126.
Graff Monument (Illustration), 179.

Grand Opera House, 126.
Grant's Cottage, 184.
Green Hill Presbyterian Church, 137.
Green Street Entrance to Park (Illustration), 181.
Greenwood Cemetery, 156.
Guarantee Trust Company, 66.
Guarantee Trust Company (Illustr'n), 67.

H.

Haddington, District of, 175.
Haddonfield, Borough of, 228.
Hahnemann Medical College and Hospital, 27.
Hahnemann Medical College (Illus.), 28.
Hale Building, 39.
Hale Building (Illustration), 38.
Hammonton, Town of, 228.
Handel and Haydn Hall, 80.
Harrison Brothers' Paint-Works, 117.
Haseltine Art Rooms, 53.
Haverford College, 216.
Hayes Mechanics' Home, 218.
Hestonville, District of, 175.
Historical Society (Catholic), 73.
Historical Society of Pennsylvania, 106.
Holmesburg, District of, 157.
Holy Trinity Parish House, 83.
Holy Trinity School, 75.
Home for Aged and Infirm Colored Persons, 174.
Home for Aged and Infirm Israelites, 211.
Home for Aged and Infirm Methodists, 127.
Home for Aged Couples, 138.
Home for Aged Couples of the Presbyterian Church, 175.
Home for Consumptives, 150, 220.
Home for Convalescents, 174, 217.
Home for Destitute Colored Children, 170.
Home for Incurables, Eliza Cathcart, 217.
Home for Incurables, Philadelphia, 170.
Home for Infants, Philadelphia, 174.

INDEX. 235

Home for Orphans of Odd-Fellows, 131.
Home for Orphans of Odd-Fellows (Illustration), 130.
Home for the Aged of Both Sexes, 137, 213.
Home of the Merciful Saviour for Crippled Children, 170.
Hood, Foulkrod & Co.'s Store, 53.
Hoopes & Townsend Bolt-Works, 121.
Horstmann's (W. H.) Military-Goods Works, 81.
Horticultural Hall, West Park, 190.
Horticultural Hall, Pennsylvania, 104.
Hospital for the Insane, 174.
Hospital of the Good Shepherd, 171, 217.
Hotels, Location of, 15.
House of Correction, 157.
House of Mercy (P. E.), 149.
House of Refuge, 137, 225.
House of the Good Shepherd, 173.
House of the Guardian Angel, 171.
Howard Hospital and Infirmary, 108.
Howard Institution, 131.
Hunting Park, 208.

I.

Independence Hall, 56.
Independence Hall (Illustration), 57.
Independence National Bank, 63.
Independence Square, 58.
Indigent Widows' and Single Women's Asylum, 170.
Insurance Company of the State of Pennsylvania, 69.
Insurance Company of North America, 69.
International Navigation Company, 149.
Introduction, Descriptive and Historical, 7.

J.

Jefferson Medical College and Hospital, 48, 108.
Jefferson Square, 151.
Jenkintown, Village of, 211.

Jewish Foster Home, 213.
Jewish Hospital Association, 208.
Joan of Arc Equestrian Statue, 184.
Journalists' Club, 107.

K.

Kalion Chemical Company, 117.
Keneseth-Israel Synagogue, 126.
Kensington, District of, 152.
Kensington Hospital for Women, 153.
Keystone Knitting-Mills, 154.
Keystone Saw-Works, 157.
Keystone Watch-Case Factory, 138.
Kirkbride's Hospital (Insane), 174.

L.

Land Title and Trust Company, 60.
Land Title and Trust Co. (Illustration), 61.
Landreth Seed Farm, 163.
Lansdowne Drive (Illustration), 188.
La Salle College, 125.
Laurel Hill Cemetery, 195.
Laurel Hill Cemetery (Illustration of South Entrance), 196.
Laurel Hill Cemetery (Illustration of North Entrance), 198.
Law Association Library, 73.
Lazaretto, 161.
League Island Navy-Yard, 160.
Lemon Hill, 182.
Letitia House (Penn Mansion), 189.
Lincoln Institution, 52.
Lincoln Monument, 182.
Lincoln Monument (Illustration), 183.
Lincoln Park, 161.
Lippincott (J. B.) Company's Book-Store, 53.
Lippincott (J. B.) Company's Book-Store (Illustration), 55.
Little Sisters of the Poor, 137.
Liverpool and London Globe Insurance Company, 69.

INDEX.

Logan Square, 93.
Lu Lu Temple, 123.
Lutheran Orphans' Home, 213.
Lutheran Theological Seminary, 213.
Lying-in Charity, 51.

M.

MacKellar, Smiths & Jordan's Type-Foundries, 62.
McKeone Soap-Works, 182.
Maennerchor Society, 79.
Maennerchor, Young, 78.
Maennerchor, Young (Illustration), 78.
Magdalen Society, 98.
Manayunk, Suburb of, 199.
Manual Training-School, 122.
Manufacturers' Club, 35.
Marcus Hook, Village of, 162.
Mary J. Drexel Home, 135.
Mary J. Drexel Home (Illustration), 136.
Masonic Home, 128.
Masonic Home (Illustration), 127.
Masonic Temple, 20.
Masonic Temple (Illustration), 23.
Master Builders' Exchange, 60.
Maternity Hospital, University, 166.
Mathilde Adler Loeb Dispensary, 211.
Media, Borough of, 224.
Medico-Chirurgical College and Hospital, 98.
Medico-Chirurgical College and Hospital (Illustration), 99.
Memorial Hall, 191.
Memorial Hall (Illustration), 191.
Mercantile Library, 48.
Merchants' Exchange, 69.
Merchantville, Borough of, 228.
Merion Cricket Club, 216.
Mermaid Inn, 214.
Mermaid Inn (Illustration), 214.
Methodist Book-Rooms, 36.
Methodist Episcopal Hospital, 110.
Methodist Hospital (Illustration), 112.
Methodist Episcopal Orphanage, 219.
Methodist Home, 128.
Midvale Steel-Works, 208.
Mifflin Square, 151.
Millville, City of, 228.
Mint (United States), 36.
Mint, United States (Illustration), 37.
Monument Cemetery, 126.
Moorestown, Village of, 228.
Morgue, Philadelphia, 141.
Morris (Robert) Residence, 182.
Mount Airy, District of, 213.
Mount Auburn Cemetery, 156.
Mount Holly, City of, 228.
Mount Moriah Cemetery, 221.
Mount Peace Cemetery, 197.
Mount Pleasant Mansion, 186.
Mount Vernon Cemetery, 197.
Moyamensing Prison, 113.
Moyamensing Prison (Illustration), 114.
Muhr's Sons' (H.) Jewelry-Works, 30.
Municipal Hospital, 128.
Musical Fund Hall, 75.
Mutual Life Insurance Company, 48.
Mutual Life Insurance Co. (Illustr'n), 49.

N.

National Bank of Commerce, 143.
National Bank of the Republic, 66.
National Bank of the Republic (Illus.), 68.
Naval Asylum and Hospital (U. S.), 115, 116.
Naval Asylum and Hospital, U. S. (Illustration), 115.
New Century Club, 39.
New Century Club (Illustration), 40.
New Jerusalem Church, 85.
New Jerusalem Church (Illustration), 87.
Newspaper Offices, 17.
Nicetown, Suburb of, 208.
Nixon's (W.) Paper-Mills, 199.

INDEX. 237

Norris Square, 153.
Norristown, City of, 215.
North Pennsylvania R. R. Station, 154.
Northern Home for Friendless Children, 137.
Northern Saving-Fund, 79.
Nurses' Home, University, 166.

O.

Odd-Fellows' Cemetery, 197.
Odd-Fellows' Hall, 25.
Odd-Fellows' Hall (Illustration), 26.
Odd-Fellows' Home, 131.
Odd-Fellows' Home (Illustration), 129.
Ogontz School for Young Ladies, 211.
Ogontz School (Illustr'n, West Wing), 209.
Ogontz School (Illustr'n, East Tower), 210.
Oil Refineries, 118.
Old Ladies' Home of Philadelphia, 156.
Old Man's Home, 171.
Old Pine Street Church, 147.
Old Swedes' Church, 149.
Old Swedes' Church (Illustr'n), 150.
Orange Street Friends' Meeting, 75.
Orphan Asylum, Burd, 175.
Orphan Asylum, Philadelphia, 175.
Orthopaedic Hospital, Philadelphia, 98.

P.

Palmyra, Village of, 229.
Paschalville, Suburb of, 172.
Passyunk Square, 113.
Pencoyd Iron-Works, 215.
Penn Asylum, 154.
Penn Club, 75.
Penn Mansion, 189.
Penn Mutual Life Insurance Company, 46.
Penn Mutual Life Insurance Co. (Illus.), 47.
Penn National Bank, 62.
Penn Treaty Monument and Square, 153.
Penn Treaty Monument (Illustration), 153.

Penn's Manor, 163.
Pennsylvania Bible Society, 73.
Pennsylvania College of Dental Surgery, 52.
Pennsylvania Historical Society, 106.
Pennsylvania Hospital, 76.
Pennsylvania Hospital for the Insane, 174.
Pennsylvania Industrial Home for Blind Women, 174.
Pennsylvania Institution for the Deaf and Dumb, 213.
Pennsylvania Institution for the Instruction of the Blind, 98.
Pennsylvania Life and Trust Company, 58.
Pennsylvania Life and Trust Company (Illustration), 59.
Pennsylvania Military College, 221.
Pennsylvania Military College (Illustrations), 222, 223.
Pennsylvania Museum and School of Industrial Art, 121.
Pennsylvania R. R. Company, 70, 144, 216.
Pennsylvania R. R. Station (Broad Street), 31.
Pennsylvania Retreat for Blind Mutes, 173.
Pennsylvania Training-School for Feeble-Minded Children, 224.
People's (State) Bank, 65.
Peters's (Judge) Residence, Belmont, 193.
Philadelphia Abattoir, 176.
Philadelphia and Atlantic City R. R. Co., 141, 208.
Philadelphia and Reading R. R. Company, 70, 141, 208.
Philadelphia and Reading Terminal Station (Illustration), 42.
Philadelphia and Reading R. R. Wharf Station (Illustration), 140.
Philadelphia Art Club, 102.
Philadelphia Art Club (Illustration), 103.
Philadelphia Base-Ball Park, 128.
Philadelphia Board of Trade, 63.
Philadelphia Bourse, 62.

Philadelphia City Institute, 85.
Philadelphia Club, 106.
Philadelphia College of Pharmacy, 51.
Philadelphia College of Pharmacy (Illustration), 50.
Philadelphia Dental College, 98.
Philadelphia Dispensary, 75.
Philadelphia Home for Incurables, 170.
Philadelphia Home for Infants, 174.
Philadelphia Hospital, 167.
Philadelphia Library, 104.
Philadelphia Library (Illustration), 105.
Philadelphia Library (Ridgway Branch), 108.
Philadelphia Library, Ridgway Branch (Illustration), 109.
Philadelphia Market, 169.
Philadelphia National Bank, 65.
Philadelphia Orphan Asylum, 175.
Philadelphia Polyclinic and College for Graduates in Medicine, 91.
Philadelphia Saving-Fund, 73.
Philadelphia Saving-Fund (Illustr'n), 74.
Philadelphia School of Design for Women, 125.
Philadelphia Society for Employment of the Poor, 151.
Philadelphia Stock Exchange, 63.
Philadelphia Trust Company, 65.
Philopatrian Hall and Literary Institute, 107.
Philosophical Society, American, 58.
Point Breeze Driving-Park, 113.
Point Breeze Gas-Works, 117.
Port Richmond, 155.
Port Richmond Grain Elevator, 155.
Post-Office (United States), 45.
Powelton Avenue Station, 176.
Powers & Weightman's Chemical Works, 80, 199.
Presbyterian Board of Publication, 35.
Presbyterian Home for Widows and Single Women, 171.
Presbyterian Hospital, 173.
Presbyterian Orphanage, 171.
Preston Retreat, 100.
Produce National Bank, 143.
Provident Building, 65.
Provident Life and Trust Company, 65.

Q.

Quaker City Cold Storage Company, 146.
Queen Lane, 220.

R.

Radnor, Village of, 217.
Railroad Stations and Offices, 18.
Reading R. R. Terminal Station, 41.
Reading R. R. Terminal Station (Illus.), 42.
Real Estate Investment Company, 73.
Real Estate Trust Company, 39.
Record Building, 46.
Record Building (Illustration), 45.
Red Bank, Village of, 161.
Red Bank Sanitarium, 161.
Reformed Episcopal Church (Second), 85.
Residence near Logan Station (Illus.), 207.
Residence, West Walnut Street (Illus.), 90.
Richmond, District of, 155.
Richmond Coal Wharves (Illustr'n), 155.
Ridgway Branch of Philadelphia Library, 108.
Ridgway Branch of Philadelphia Library (Illustration), 109.
Ridley Park, Village of, 221.
Rittenhouse Club, 85.
Rittenhouse Square, 83.
Rittenhouse Square (Illustration), 84.
Riverside, Village of, 162.
Riverton, Village of, 162.
Roach's Ship-Yard, 161.
Rodef Shalom Synagogue, 123.
Roman Catholic Cathedral, 93.
Roman Catholic Cathedral (Illustr'n), 92.
Rosine Association, 100.
Roxborough, Suburb of, 199.

Royal Insurance Company, 69.
Rush Hospital for Consumptives, 91.

S.

St. Agnes's Hospital, 110.
St. Agnes's Hospital (Illustration), 111.
St. Asaph's Church, 219.
St. Charles Borromeo, Seminary of, 216.
St. Christopher's Hospital for Children, 154.
St. David's Church, 217.
St. George's Hall, 30.
St. James's Church, 171.
St. Joseph's Church, 70.
St. Joseph's College, 137.
St. Joseph's Female Orphan Asylum, 75.
St. Joseph's Hospital, 137.
St. Mary's Church, 70.
St. Mary's Hospital, 154.
St. Paul's Church (P. E.), 70.
St. Peter's Church, 147.
St. Vincent's Home, 94.
Salem, City of, 228.
Samaritan Hospital (Baptist), 128.
Sanitarium, Children's, 161.
School Lane, 199, 220.
School of Design for Women, 125.
Schuylkill Arsenal, 116.
Schuylkill Falls Bluff (Illustration), 186.
Schuylkill Navy, 184.
Schuylkill Navy Athletic Club, 97.
Schuylkill Navy Athletic Club (Illus.), 96.
Seamen's Friend Society, 150.
Seamen's Missionary Association, 151.
Seaside House for Invalid Women, 230.
Seaside Resorts, Railroads to, 228.
Sellers (Wm.) & Co., Machine-Works, 119.
Shad-Fishing at Gloucester (Illus.), 146.
Signal Service (U. S.), 45.
Simpson Print-Works, 161.
Sketch Club, Philadelphia, 107.
Soldiers' and Sailors' Orphans' Home, 137.
Southern Home for Destitute Children, 110.

Spring Garden Institute, 121.
Spring Garden Water-Works, 185.
Star Braid-Works, 182.
State in Schuylkill Club, 162.
Steamboat Lines, 139.
Stock Exchange, Philadelphia, 63.
Strawberry Mansion, 187.
Strawbridge & Clothier's Store, 53.
Sugar Trust Refineries, 148.
Sunday Breakfast Association, 51.
Supreme Court (State), 19.
Swarthmore College, 224.
Sweet Brier from Egglesfield (Illus.), 189.

T.

Tabernacle Presbyterian Church, 169.
Tacony, District of, 157.
Tammany Fish-House, 162.
Tam O'Shanter Group of Statuary, 184.
Taylor's Tin-Plate Works, 148.
Telegraph and Telephone Offices, 18.
Temple College, 126.
Temporary Home Association, 79.
Terminal Station (P. & R. R. R.), 41.
Terminal Station (Illustration), 42.
Theatres, Location of, 16.
Third Presbyterian Church, 147.
Tinicum Island, 161.
Torresdale, District of, 162.
Tradesmen's National Bank, 63.
Trenton, City of, 163.
Trinity P. E. Church (Old), 157.
Tullytown, Village of, 163.

U.

Union Benevolent Association, 75.
Union Insurance Company, 69.
Union League of Philadelphia, 33.
Union League of Philadelphia (Illus.), 34.
Union Trust Company, 60.
Unitarian Church (First), 85.

Unitarian Club, 107.
United States Appraiser's Building, 143.
United States Court-Rooms, 19, 56.
United States Custom-House, 65.
United States Custom-House (Illus.), 66.
United States Mint, 36.
United States Mint (Illustration), 37.
United States Naval Asylum and Hospital, 115, 116.
United States Naval Asylum and Hospital (Illustration), 115.
United States Post-Office, 45.
United States Post-Office (Illustr'n), 44.
University Club, 107.
University Hospital, 164.
University Law School, 33.
University of Pennsylvania, 164.
University of Pennsylvania (Illus.), 165.

V.

Veterinary College and Hospital of University, 164.
Veterinary College (Illustration), 166.
Valley Forge, 215.
Valley Green Hotel (Illustration), 205.
Villa Nova College and Monastery, 217.
View above Sweet Brier (Illustr'n), 190.
Vineland, Village of. 228.

W.

Wagner Free Institute of Science, 131.
Wakefield Mills, 211.
Wakefield Mills (Illustration), 212.
Wallingford, Village of, 224.
Wanamaker Grand Depot, 36.
Walk to Strawberry Mansion (Illus.), 187.
Washington Monument, 230.
Washington Monument (Illustr'n), 229.
Washington Square, 73.
Wayne, Borough of, 217.
Wayne Junction, 208.

West Chester, Borough of, 226.
West Jersey Railroad, 139, 228.
West Laurel Hill Cemetery, 219.
West (Benjamin) House, 224.
Western Home for Poor Children, 174.
Western National Bank, 65.
Western Temporary Home, 174.
Westtown School, 226.
Whelen Home for Girls, 97.
White (S. S.) Dental Manufacturing Company, 39.
Whitney Car-Wheel Works, 119.
William Penn Charter School, 41.
Williamson Free School of Mechanical Trades, 224.
Wills Eye Hospital, 97.
Wilmington, City of, 162.
Wissahickon Creek, 201.
Wissahickon Creek (Illustration), 202.
Wissahickon, View of the (Illustr'n), 204.
Wissahickon Drive (Illustration), 203.
Wissahickon Inn, 206, 220.
Woman's Christian Temperance Union, 30.
Woman's Medical College and Hospital, 135.
Women's Christian Association, 97.
Women's Christian Association (Illus.), 95.
Women's Homœopathic Hospital, 128.
Wood (R. D.), Building, 65.
Wood (Wm.) & Co.'s Pequea Mills, 182.
Woodbury, City of, 228.
Woodland Cemetery, 167.
Working Home for Blind Men, 173.

Y.

Young Maennerchor Society, 78.
Young Men's Christian Association, 35.

Z.

Zoological Garden, 176.

www.ingramcontent.com/pod-product-compliance
Lightning Source LLC
Chambersburg PA
CBHW031735230426
43669CB00007B/351